CLASSROOM
STRUGGLES

CLASSROOM STRUGGLES

EDUCATION REPORTING AND ANALYSIS FROM TRANSITIONS

PREFACE BY JEREMY DRUKER

**EXECUTIVE DIRECTOR AND
EDITOR IN CHIEF AT TRANSITIONS**

**EDITED AND WITH A FOREWORD
BY TIMOTHY SPENCE**

TOL

PRAGUE › NEW YORK

Cover design by Cosimo/www.popshopstudio.com
Cover photo by Janos Kummer
Interior layout by Cosimo/www.popshopstudio.com

ISBN: 978-0-98360-210-1

Ordering Information:
Transitions publications are available at online bookstores. They may also be purchased for educational, business, or promotional use.
Bulk orders: Special discounts are available on bulk orders for reading groups, organizations, businesses, and others.

For more information, contact us at:

Transitions
P.O. Box 416, Old Chelsea Station
New York, NY 10011

tol@cosimobooks.com

Visit us online at:
http://www.tol.org

or visit the Transitions Online Chalkboard at:
http://chalkboard.tol.org

CONTENTS

I. HISTORY 101

Reasonable Doubt? Some young Russians have heard so many
lies from their government that they can no longer tell real heroism
from fakery.

Getting Its Story Straight: Efforts to teach a national history
in Montenegro lead to a familiar minefield.

Two Histories of One Homeland: Tbilisi blocks books that
teach an Armenia-centric version of history in a border area.

Teaching One History, Living Another: Correspondents in
Bulgaria, the Czech Republic, Hungary, Poland, Romania,
and Slovakia asked history teachers to describe their
working life today compared with conditions before 1989.

II. POST-CONFLICT LESSONS

III. THE PRIVILEGED CLASS

IV. PRIDE AND PREJUDICE

V. LANGUAGE LAB

VI. PROGRESS REPORT

VII. ACHIEVERS

PREFACE

The origins of this book date to 2004, when I met Natalia Shablya, a young Ukrainian education expert, at a restaurant in Budapest to discuss the media's role in putting education issues higher on the public agenda.

Over the course of some fine Hungarian food, Natalia, a program manager for the Open Society Foundations' Education Support Program (OSF-ESP), expressed her frustration over the paucity of good reporting on education across the post-communist region, and how few journalists really knew the ins and outs of the "beat." And, I learned, even when intrepid reporters took the time to understand education reform and the specialist terminology, their articles would almost invariably be relegated to the back pages of their publications, with "more important" stories dominating the headlines. It could thus be pretty lonely as an education reporter.

Natalia and I started plotting out a program designed to counteract that situation, a program that has since grown into a successful partnership with ESP. Our goals have been to train journalists to report on education in a more engaging and professional manner; to offer a wide range of resources to enable journalists to improve their reporting skills; to connect education reporters across the post-communist region so they can exchange experiences and provide mutual support; and to elevate public awareness of education issues.

Along the way, we have held workshops for both aspiring and experienced education journalists; created an education resource site (http://chalkboard.tol.org); introduced the region's first distance-learning course on education reporting; and published dozens of education-related articles in our first three years. We have also started to expand the scope of those activities beyond the former-Soviet bloc into Africa and Asia.

None of this would have been possible without OSF's support and the dedication of the staff at Transitions. I would first like to thank Natalia for her vision in launching the project, and her colleagues who have nurtured it since those early days: Piroska Hugyecz, Nora Henter, Ian Macpherson, and the ESP director, Hugh McLean. Veteran journalism trainer Linda Christmas deserves much credit for her work, online and in person, with many of the program's past participants.

At Transitions, much appreciation goes to former project manager, Kristy Ironside, and past and current editors Andy Markowitz, Barbara Frye, and Ky Krauthamer for their tireless work in improving the quality of the content presented in this book, and passing along tips and advice to our contributors to help them improve their journalism skills. I left out former Managing Editor Timothy Spence from that list, only to offer special thanks for taking over this book project and making it a reality.

There can never be enough quality reporting on education, and we are proud to have provided support to a growing group of journalists who feel the same way. Please enjoy the results of their endeavors.

— *Jeremy Druker*

FOREWORD

Education shall be directed to the full development of the
human personality and to the strengthening of respect for
human rights and fundamental freedoms. It shall promote
understanding, tolerance and friendship among all nations, racial or
religious groups, and shall further the activities of the United Nations
for the maintenance of peace.
— *Universal Declaration of Human Rights, Article 26*

Intolerance, manipulation, and cultural hegemony. These surely were what the authors of the Universal Declaration of Human Rights intended to avoid, but the universe is not so perfect as the brave vision written in 1948.

The Cold War's end may have knocked down barriers, but not blinders, and that is as true in the classroom as it is in seats of power. In Russia, academic and educational institutions that rock the boat face censure if not outright closure. Top educators are expected to swear fealty to the ruling party or find another job.

In other countries where expression is restricted, policymakers prescribe what textbooks will say, how history will be viewed, or what language will predominate even in multicultural societies.

Classroom Struggles exposes these and other roadblocks through news and feature articles drawn from correspondent reports published by Transitions, founded in 1999, and its companion education website, TOL Chalkboard. This collection highlights some of the best reporting and analysis in the first three years of Chalkboard, launched in 2008 to spotlight the education reporting of young journalists. It focuses on Transitions' traditional coverage areas—Eastern Europe and the Balkans, the Caucasus, Central Asia, and Russia—with the added insights of Chalkboard contributors in other regions.

Compendiums of journalists' works are not uncommon, be it a

photojournalist's picture book or a war correspondent's bound dispatches. Where this compendium breaks ground is that it gives an outlet to those who don't have a voice or are willfully overlooked in education policy—disenfranchised minorities or teachers, parents, and students who are denied the freedom to complain.

As Galina Stolyarova and Andrea Gregory report in their thoughtfully written articles in the opening chapter, politicians in the post-communist sphere continue to dabble at doctoring history, leaving students better educated in cynicism than in their past. "Ultimately, if people are losing any connection with the history of their own country, it is people's stories, and certainly not the false promises of officials, that can restore it," Transitions' longtime correspondent and columnist Stolyarova says of the modern, wildly distorted interpretations of the Leningrad siege during World War II.

Gregory's "Getting Its Story Straight" describes the minefield Montenegrin policymakers created in trying to craft a past for a new nation that history teachers find implausible. Tamar Kikacheishvili writes in "Cultivating a Martial Spirit" about the Georgian government's attempt to push coursework in "military patriotism" following the country's humiliating defeat by Russia in their 2008 border war.

Wars leave raw wounds in every society, but they can be especially disruptive to the most vulnerable—children. As field reports from Afghanistan and the West African nation of Liberia drive home, internecine fighting has left children in those countries without basic tools of learning.

The impact on children is also highlighted in the 2010 unrest in Kyrgyzstan, which exposed the neglect of education left by the ousted president Kurmanbek Bakiev, as Hamid Toursunov reports from one of the country's conflict-prone regions in "Jumping off a Sinking Ship."

Language presents a different struggle. From Central Asia to Eastern Europe, the "Balkanization" of language grows ever deeper, fueling nationalism and resentment, and pitting neighbor against neighbor.

Signs of neglect and budget woes are everywhere, leading in some cases to unorthodox solutions. Correspondent Ljubica Grozdanovska Dimishkovska reports in "Macabre Market" on how Macedonian medical students resort to back-alley deals to buy skeletons for their studies because of insufficient resources at their university.

And yet the scene is not altogether one of graft, distortion, or macabre moments. Hungarian journalist Anita Komuves reports, in "Hard Cases," on a promising program aimed at the young outcasts of Hungary's public education who are finding new opportunity at "BT." The Budapest school is giving its students a chance to complete a secondary education, and the hope for university admission. In South Africa, generations of adults denied schooling because of their skin color are returning to the classroom for an education once thought beyond reach. South African journalist A'Eysha Kassiem writes about one such school near Cape Town in "A Second Chance."

Change for the better does happen, as Dorota Ochal says in "Teaching One History, Living Another." Looking back to the Eastern European revolutions of 1989, the retired Polish history teacher recalls the irony of unexpected freedom. "It was that history ceased to have the taste of a forbidden fruit. It became just another lesson. It may sound strange from a history teacher, but I think that's good. Things returned to their proper order."

Proper order is messy, which makes this collection all the more compelling as a source for understanding, discussion, and perhaps even as a tool to pry open closed minds.

It may also be a useful tool to journalists, who aren't always keen to take an education beat on the assumption that it is not fraught with enough career-advancing drama. The ensuing reports demonstrate that being assigned to cover education is anything but a dead end.

— *Timothy Spence*

I. HISTORY 101

REASONABLE DOUBT?

By Galina Stolyarova

Some young Russians have heard so many lies from their government that they can no longer tell real heroism from fakery.

ST. PETERSBURG

Russian television was full of pomp and solemnity on the 65th anniversary of the lifting of the siege of Leningrad during World War II.[1] It offered the predictable pageantry, complete with the inevitable ultra-detailed coverage of President Dmitry Medvedev attending events in the city.

In Russian cyberspace, the scene was very different. Bloggers slammed the siege of Leningrad as a propaganda myth, expressing a strong anti-Russian sentiment and suggesting that the lives lost during the siege would not have been worth saving anyway. The siege, in other words, was a sort of a necessary cleansing, they claimed.

One blogger commenting on LiveJournal dismissed the posters of archive photographs documenting the siege as "bloody Photoshop," while another said the siege merely enabled "the disposal of human trash." Several bloggers cheerfully agreed that Russia was always weak and the siege was lifted solely because the Germans were no longer interested, while the heroic breaking of the siege was nothing more than "wretched propaganda" and "a lingering Soviet myth."

The tone in which the bloggers dismissed the alleged Photoshop images echoed the way some young people comment on the improbably perfect bodies of models in glossy magazines.

Only the lowest of the low would ridicule war veterans. But perhaps this attitude shows that too much around these young people is fake and false. Perhaps they simply have heard too many lies.

Don't Believe It

On television, top Russian officials took turns praising the heroic deeds of the siege veterans. Yet shortly before the anniversary, the city government canceled discounts on household utility bills for several categories of people, including siege survivors. It is an open secret that in Russia most war veterans live in devastating poverty and often reflect among themselves—never on television, of course—that, in a sense, they lost the war. Misery and meager state pensions are what the authorities awarded war veterans. Now cynical young people doubt their role in winning the war.

While the notorious hypocrisy of the authorities has played a role in the growing cynicism of Russian society, ignorance of history has not helped.

That ignorance is hardly surprising, considering that the official history curriculum in Russian high schools devotes a mere five academic hours to World War II. Most knowledge of the war therefore comes from television or Internet forums.

Indeed, Russians see so much hypocrisy every day that they are beginning to regard with suspicion even those things that have been considered sacrosanct, the siege of Leningrad being a perfect example. Everything is now being seen through the prism of the hypocrisy of the authorities. Ultimately, it is not the value of the heroic achievement that was being questioned in the forums. Rather it was a sign that trust in the authorities has long been undermined and so whatever the authorities talk about with pride has to be treated with contempt. So much brainwashing and propaganda airs on Russian television that the pompous coverage of the siege anniversary gets the same kind of reception in some quarters. The value of the victory gets tuned out along with the excessive propaganda.

So television has been ruined as an authentic means of commemoration. What might take its place? Human stories, perhaps, like that of trombonist Viktor Orlovsky, who performed at the Leningrad premiere of Dmitry Shostakovich's Seventh Symphony on 9 August 1942. Orlovsky told me that if a member of Leningrad's Bolshoi Symphony Orchestra didn't show up at a rehearsal during the first months of 1942, fellow musicians would begin to feel a familiar nausea. They knew that nobody would pick up the phone when they rang the absentee—and that a rescue brigade sent to the home would find the musician dead.

The original idea behind the creation of the orchestra of musicians who remained in the city was to bring hope to Leningraders living without electricity and heating. At that time, the only sounds coming out of street-mounted loudspeakers were air-raid warnings and subsequent all-clear signals.

Although the members of the orchestra received additional rations to be able to go on stage and perform, their physical condition wasn't much better than that of the average citizen.

Orlovsky remembered cutting the edges of his *valenki*, or felt boots, to be able to get his swollen feet into them.

With winter temperatures below minus 30 degrees Celsius and no electricity or heating during the second winter of the siege, the orchestra's pianist, Alexander Kamensky, kept his hands warm by placing two scorching bricks on both sides of the instrument to radiate some heat. Conductor Karl Eliasberg was so weak he was driven to rehearsals on a sledge.

Many years after the war, Eliasberg was approached by a group of German tourists who had once been on the other side of the barricades listening to his orchestra playing Shostakovich. The Germans were close enough to the city to be able to catch the Leningrad radio signals that carried many of the orchestra's concerts.

They came to St. Petersburg specifically to tell the musician that back on that day in August 1942, they knew they would never take Leningrad. Because, they said, there was a factor more important than starvation, fear, and death.

If such testimonies, rather than the hypocritical statements of the officials, were the focal point of the war anniversaries, there would probably be less denial in society.

The orchestra gave 300 performances during the nearly 900 days of the siege, but the performance of Shostakovich's Seventh Symphony was special.

Hitler had planned a banquet at the city's Astoria Hotel on 9 August, the day of the performance. But not only had the Germans not entered the city, not a single bomb fell on the Philharmonic on that night, although the hall was lit up.

"There were no curtains, and the light was pouring out of the windows," Orlovsky said. "People in the audience were squinting, as they had gotten used to life without electric light. ... Everyone was dressed up and some even had their hair done. The atmosphere was so festive and optimistic it felt like a victory."

Eliasberg received a bouquet of flowers from a teenage girl who said her family did this because "life had to go on as usual whatever is happening around us."

The musicians didn't know that the Soviet Army had stepped up its shelling of German positions to protect the building during the performance.

Russia's culture minister, Alexander Avdeyev, has been complaining about what he sees as a "devastating lack of patriotism" and recently announced a plan to fund "patriotic films." Specific ideas were lacking, however. The minister, for one, voiced none.

Why not make a film about the pianist Kamensky or the conductor Eliasberg?

Ultimately, if people are losing any connection with the history of their own country, it is people's stories, and certainly not the false promises of officials, that can restore it.

Transitions Online, 5 February 2009

GETTING
ITS STORY
STRAIGHT

By Andrea Gregory[2]

*Efforts to teach a national history in Montenegro
lead to a familiar minefield.*

PODGORICA

Predrag Raznatovic quickly reads aloud through the part of the history book that states thousands of Montenegrins were killed by Serbs in 1918. He doesn't believe what he is saying, but he reads it anyway. He is a history teacher.

Raznatovic, a teacher for 15 years, uses a relatively new textbook to teach the history of a relatively new country. Although he acknowledges that a history textbook is "a stamp of its time," he argues that "the main agenda of education should be education."

The history teacher and other critics of the new books say they sideline world figures in order to focus on Montenegro, and that they distort the history of Serbia, with which Montenegro formed a federation for nearly a century.

The books' defenders, however, say they are a good-faith attempt to shine a light on Montenegro's long-overlooked national history.

'About Ideology'

"These school books are not good for our situation," Raznatovic said. "It's not good for the future of the relationships between Montenegro and Serbia. ... Nationalism is always a really big danger."

Alen Abdomerovic disagrees. At 20, Abdomerovic was born as Yugoslavia began to dissolve, and the history he learned changed along with the circumstances. Now a proud citizen of a newly independent Montenegro, he said a certain amount of nationalism is appropriate in a country trying to define itself.

Arguing that Serb nationalism swept through the region in the early 1990s, he said, "Now it is Montenegrin nationalism. I think it's OK for now."

Nor does he have a problem with that nationalism being promoted in textbooks. "I think it's OK. I think every book you write, it's good to write pro-something or anti-something to promote something," he said.

Serbia and Montenegro went their separate ways in 2006, after a majority of Montenegrins approved an independence referendum. In October 2007, Montenegro adopted a new constitution and national anthem. It has also designated the official language Montenegrin and created an official history.

Raznatovic said he favors an independent Montenegro but fears that changing the textbooks and the name of the language were "a dangerous way to build a new nation."

A greater focus on Montenegro's past in the new books has meant a significantly abbreviated survey of world history, the teacher said. He cites the deletion of lessons for second- and third-graders about Russia's formation and its towering historical figures, such as Peter the Great.

Members of the Serbian People's Party, say the new books are part of a wave of anti-Serbian sentiment being fomented by the government. "It's not a matter of science at all. It's about ideology," party spokesman Dobrilo Dedeic said, arguing that the changes are aimed at chipping away at young ethnic Serbs' identification with Serbia.

He singled out the treatment of the Jasenovac concentration camp in Croatia during World War II. "Historical facts say that 600,000 Serbs were killed in Jasenovac. In history books in Montenegro the figures are different and copied from the Croatian books. The Croats strongly minimized the number of murdered Serbs."

The *Encyclopedia of the Holocaust*, published by the U.S. Holocaust Memorial Museum, states, "It is presently estimated that the Ustasa [fascist] regime murdered between 56,000 and 97,000 people in Jasenovac between 1941 and 1945."

The Right Balance

Biljana Miranovic, an editor at Education Ministry who supervised the publication of the new textbooks, defended them. She said that before Montenegro established its own education bureaucracy in 2001, "Our students used to learn history from books written and published in Belgrade. The percentage of Montenegrin national history, in comparison to the rest, was not more than 8 percent." The new books devote more than 40 percent of their content to national history.

Still, in shifting the focus, Miranovic said the ministry has been sensitive to Montenegro's patchwork of identities. "Our citizens have different national and political backgrounds and we were aware of that. We tried, and I think succeeded, to reach that balance. Our history books don't glorify any of existing nationalities."

Slavko Burzanovic, one of the authors of the history textbooks, has little patience with the critics. "The most dissatisfied are those who don't believe in the existence of the Montenegrin nation (or Macedonian, Albanian, and Bosnian)—those for whom it is a painful and unacceptable fact that Montenegro exists," he said. "The fact that the majority in Montenegro don't share their ideology is something they will call anti-Serbian politics."

But efforts to assert a Montenegrin identity necessarily require drawing distinctions between Montenegro and Serbia. It is a touchy business, despite the peaceful breakup of their union. Their peoples share a common language, whether called Montenegrin or Serbian, and the Orthodox faith. Many families have relatives on either side of the border.

When in the fall of 2007 the Education Ministry declared Montenegrin to be the official name of the language used in schools, 12 teachers in Niksic resigned. The ministry had tried to ease into the renaming of the language by referring to it as the native tongue, when independence was first on the horizon.

"Austria never said, 'I don't like Germany so my language is not German,'" history teacher Raznatovic said.

Wanted: Cooler Heads

Igor Milosevic, executive director of the Podgorica-based Association for Democratic Prosperity, a nongovernmental organization with a strong focus on regional cooperation, complains that the region is far more interested in the past than the future.

"It is part of a political game. Winners write the history," Milosevic said.

When he was in school in the 1980s, two years of national history lessons were dominated by Serbia's history, with very little mention of Montenegro, he said. Now the tables have turned.

"Ten years ago, the government had one approach, and now they have a completely different approach," he said.

History, language, and national songs are all components of a country's identity, Milosevic concedes, but he worries that the Montenegrin government is rushing things.

"You cannot change identity under pressure. Our government doesn't know how to approach without pressure," he said.

The job of writing Balkan history may be best done by outside experts or independent think tanks, Milosevic said. And he believes it is possible for neighboring countries to accept one history text.

History books throughout the Balkans recount different versions of the region's recent past. "Probably we need to decide what happened," Milosevic said. "If we continue to work this way, we'll probably have another war. We can't speak of our own conflict from one point of view, while Croatia speaks about it from their point of view."

Aleksandar Stamatovic, a pro-Serb historian who lives in Montenegro, said every student in the Balkans should learn one true history, difficult as that might be. Stamatovic would like to take on the job but knows that some of his claims, including that the Srebrenica massacre in Bosnia and Herzegovina was exaggerated, if not made up, would scuttle any such opportunity.

He accuses others of obscuring the truth. For example, he said, Milos Obilic was once seen as a Serb military hero who fought in the Battle of Kosovo between the Serbian and the Ottoman empires in 1389. Montenegro's new official history declares him a fairy-tale figure, Stamatovic said.

"By saying he is a legendary character, a mythological character, with these new history books, Montenegro's regime is making its own grandfathers and ancestors imbeciles," he said. "They are falsifying history or they are inventing a new one."

Stamatovic teaches history in Sarajevo. He said he cannot find work in Montenegro because of his views.

"The anti-Serbian stance in Montenegro is kind of a job now. All those who want to tell anti-Serb stories in Montenegro can find a good job and they have a good life. Those who feel ethnically and nationally like Serbs are second-class citizens, and all the doors are shut for them," Stamatovic said.

Blatant manipulation of textbooks for political aims, as practiced throughout the region, is not likely to meet much resistance in the classroom, even from savvy students.

Rastko Pajkovic, 17, said he knows better than to press his teachers for answers if something does not add up. He does not want to jeopardize his marks.

Pajkovic considers himself a Serb living in Montenegro. He said his history teacher is pro-Montenegrin but does a fair job of leaving her opinions out of the lessons. However, he is aware that his book was published in Montenegro and said it has a slant.

"I think this history was really part of creating this national identity. This is a way of de-Serbization," he said.

Transitions Online, 3 March 2008

TWO HISTORIES OF ONE HOMELAND

By Olesya Vartanyan

Tbilisi blocks books that teach an Armenia-centric version of history in a border area.

NINOTSMINDA, GEORGIA

For the second year in a row, teachers in an Armenian school in Ninotsminda, a town just inside the Georgian border, have faced the school year with a shortage of Armenian history textbooks.

"There are only two or three books for the whole class of about 20 to 25 children. How can they all properly learn what we try to teach?" said Principal Tigran Pogosyan, who is also a history teacher. He accused the Georgian Education Ministry of trying to ban the books.

Supply didn't use to be a problem. For 10 years the Armenian, not Georgian, government provided textbooks as a gift to schools in Javakheti, a border region of some 96,000 people that includes Ninotsminda and is populated mainly by ethnic Armenians.

But officials in Tbilisi, concerned over what history students here were being taught, reached a verbal agreement in 2004 with the Armenian Education Ministry that Armenia would continue to supply all the books for Javakheti schools except those on Armenian history and geography.

Teachers in Javakheti did not know of the deal, the effects of which have been felt only relatively recently, as Georgian customs operations have tightened up. In the first years of the agreement, trucks with any type of book could breeze through border posts unhindered, according to the Georgian Education Ministry.

But it came to light in summer 2007 when a truck full of Armenian history books was turned back at the border. More people began paying attention when the same thing happened the following year. In that instance, all the textbooks in the truck were allowed in except those on the history of Armenia.

David Rstkyan, co-chairman of Virk, an ethnic Armenian political party, said that the second time the books were blocked, he demanded unsuccessfully of customs agents, "Will anybody explain to us if these are the prohibited books?"

The restrictions came as the two countries have not been able to settle their differences over how to teach the history of the region.

In the late 1980s, when a strong Armenian nationalist movement started in Javakheti as the Soviet Union began to unravel, the teaching of Armenian history in local schools was one of the main demands of regional leaders.

Many residents of Javakheti don't speak Georgian and have limited contact with the rest of the country. According to a poll commissioned by the Georgian Education Ministry in 2006, nearly all the local population uses Armenian as the only language for communication.

Most local youth study and work in Armenia instead of getting an education in Georgian universities.

According to the Education Ministry's regional offices, only about 60 graduates of Armenian schools here entered Georgian universities in the last four years. By comparison, in 2008 alone there were more than 1,200 graduates in Javakheti. Hundreds started studying in Armenian institutes, the office directors say.

This failure to assimilate into Georgian culture is an especially sensitive issue in a country that is riven by various separatist movements.

Citing the use of history "to support or debunk the claims of an ethnic group" during the Soviet era, a report released in the fall by the European Center for Minority Issues, a German research organization, stated, "This trend has somewhat continued to permeate Georgian historiography and is evidenced in the discourse of leaders on ethnic disputes in the country today.

"These two tendencies, ethnocentrism and the politicization of history, are also characteristic of current practices in Georgian history teaching," the report said.

Several years ago Georgian education officials said schools in Javakheti could offer optional classes in Armenian history but provided no funding or support.

Fact or Fiction?

By that time Armenian and Georgian historians had already been in a long struggle about several facts that differ in the history textbooks of the two countries.

For example, eighth-graders in Javakheti read in the Armenian history textbook that in 1918 their region was part of Armenia and became Georgian territory only after it was invaded by the Georgian army.

The next school year these pupils would learn from the Georgian history textbook that it was the Armenian side that invaded the region and "presented claims" for their homeland, which had been a part of Georgia.

One of the touchiest questions is when Armenians came to this region. Armenian historians insist that Javakheti was originally populated by Armenians, while Georgian researchers say the Armenians were resettled there by the Russian czar two centuries ago and that the only original ethnic group was Georgians.

Differences like these bring both educational and political problems to the ethnically sensitive region. Researchers and experts on the history of the area say they know of no research that has attempted to sort out and discuss the facts presented by Armenian and Georgian historians. Children in Javakheti get either the Georgian or Armenian slant on history.

Anaid Kasoyan, 16, will graduate next year from a school in Ninotsminda. Kasoyan said she is working particularly hard to master Georgian history for her graduation exams. As for Armenian history, she said, "We never spent much time studying Armenian history. We don't have many lessons on it and not all of us have a textbook."

Simon Janashia, a former director of the national curriculum and assessment center, said the Georgian side has made two official proposals to the Armenian Education Ministry to start joint work and solve the differences, but neither was accepted.

Janashia said the ministry first proposed a commission of 10 Georgian and Armenian historians who would work out the differences.

"We were also ready to work on a combined history textbook that would reflect different points of view on controversial issues," Janashia said. He acknowledged, however, that "It has never been a priority for us."

Nune Vardanyan, a spokeswoman for the Armenian Education Ministry, said it did not receive any proposals from the Georgian side. She said the Armenian side was ready to start working jointly with its Georgian counterpart.

Teachers in Javakheti are trying to solve the problem themselves. They have asked their former pupils to find their old books and bring them to school.

"We need to learn Armenian history because we are all Armenians," Pogosyan said. "This is what we all need to understand first of all."

Kasoyan, the graduating student, said the Georgian history textbooks are written in a clearer and more interesting way. "That's why when I answer questions from my teacher, I always refer to what's written in the Georgian history textbook. But sometimes it gets too confusing and I don't know what answer is true, which book I should refer to."

Transitions Online, 15 December 2009

TEACHING ONE HISTORY, LIVING ANOTHER

By Boyko Vassilev, Lucie Kavanova, Anita Komuves,
Wojciech Kosc, Sinziana Demian, and Pavol Szalai

Correspondents in Bulgaria, the Czech Republic, Hungary, Poland,
Romania, and Slovakia asked history teachers to describe their
working life today compared with conditions before 1989.[3]

VALERY KATSUNOV, 56, BULGARIA

Katsunov is a history professor at St. Kliment Ohridski University in Sofia
and a member of the state committee for reviewing and releasing communist-era
security files.

Generally, nothing has changed.

Professionally, many plans and discussions about new textbooks took
place. At the end, no truly new textbook appeared. We repeat the old.
Variations differ according to the authors. We neither evaluated socialism
and the times of "comrade Zhivkov," nor decided where to go further—
with the EU and NATO being the notable exception.

Clichés didn't change, nor did topics. Some pale attempts were
made to have a nationally oriented history, to classify national problems,
but this went nowhere. The historians who managed to grasp the new
opportunities faster and in a pragmatic way were those who dealt with
contemporary history. They understood quickly that their writings would
determine people's perceptions. So they started to describe "comrade"
Zhivkov's time as a period of wealth, forgetting that different stages of
socialism had different levels of violence. And the younger generation's
opinions are shaped by their texts.

In the beginning students wanted something new. A group among them prevailed; it dealt predominantly with national (I do not say nationalistic) problems. Over the years this group started to disintegrate. Now students have easier curricula, but they study much less. There is a principle among professors: "Let's give a higher mark, let's not spoil his or her stipend." I graduated in 1979 and from 100 people; only five had excellent marks. Nowadays 70 percent do. Unfortunately, we constantly go below world educational standards.

The financial status of history professors in universities has changed. There was a period after the changes when we received ridiculous salaries of about $8 to $10 [per month]. Nowadays, my colleagues get one, let's say, average salary—below the country's average, but nevertheless a better one. I hope they'll get also good pensions, because today the retired historians don't. Before 1989 just a very small portion of historians (and with the blessing of State Security) traveled around the world; few of us knew what a real library looked like—in Vienna, Paris, or the Vatican. Now everyone is free to travel, provided one finds the necessary finances.

Bulgarian historians were involved with politics even before the changes. Some of them were directly connected to "comrade" Zhivkov's family and used that to make a real career in the discipline. In principle, the historian fits well everywhere. If one had studied his lessons, one could do well in various places and have balanced opinions on various topics. Everything in this world in centered on personal ambitions and on the will to prosper. I noticed that historians with bold ambitions achieved a lot scientifically through cooperating with State Security—sometimes at the expense of other colleagues. For many years history has been an ideological discipline. ... History can be a terrible or a beautiful story. Eventually, every single one of us who deals with history wants, maybe unconsciously, to leave his name on it. I think this ambition provides the reason why many historians from the older generation cooperated with State Security.

The most unpleasant thing for me was to watch some of my colleagues: those who furiously defended socialist ideology before the changes—and then turned around. It suddenly appeared that they were "oppressed"—and at once they pretended to teach history in a democratic way. It didn't work. First of all, we knew one another. And most importantly, the substance of their history lectures didn't change. ... Maybe that's why the teaching of history didn't improve.

Dana Veprakova, 53 Czech Republic

Veprkova, a high school vice principal, has been teaching since 1979.

Both before and after 1989, the content of history classes was dictated by a central educational institution. However, nowadays, we can use much more creativity in how to apply the prescribed teaching plan according to the abilities of each class.

Our teaching methods have changed dramatically. It's no longer about the student sitting in a chair with hands behind his or her back and mouth shut. There is much more mutual cooperation between the teacher and his or her students, and we practice much more teamwork.

Technologies have changed the role of teachers a lot. Where we used to be the only source of information for our students, they can check what we're telling them in many other sources these days. We can no longer claim to know the only truth, because students can very easily say, "Well, here it says something different!"

A lot of information used to be censored, so even we history teachers didn't know about some historical events. For instance, I had never heard of the Katyn massacre before 1989. Further, numerous historical personalities were misinterpreted, such as [communist Czechoslovak journalist] Julius Fucik or [medieval Czech military commander] Jan Zizka. After 1989, I discovered a lot of missing knowledge myself. That's why, shortly after the [Velvet] revolution, I attended a three-year extra study course at Charles University in order to learn about what had been hidden from us.

The Communist Party used to have tremendous influence over what was taught—they controlled the teaching plans and also organized various kinds of "training" for those who were not members of the party. We had to listen to a party representative reading from *Rude Pravo* [a party newspaper]. All teachers also had to make a yearly official declaration of what newspapers they subscribed to and if the party publication was not there, they were strongly [urged] to subscribe to it.

I tried to find a balance between following the official teaching plan and not doing propaganda for the party. So I taught the medieval era in detail, for instance, but tried not to spend as much time on modern history. Sure, I could have refused to teach about [Gustav] Husak [the then-president and Communist Party leader], for example, but I would have lost my job.

I wasn't in the Communist Party, but my options for an active fight against communism, in my classes as well, were rather limited. Nobody knew then that there would be something like 1989 and I was in the first place a mother of two children, who could have been affected by any actions of mine against the party.

A paradox is that there are still teachers who refuse to teach modern history for various reasons. Sure, it's "safer" and easier to teach about prehistory than about the '50s or '60s, because modern history is tied to many other areas, such as politics, so it requires a lot of extra study and work for the teachers. However, I believe it's important to teach modern history as well, because only then can the students understand the world around them.

My students these days are very different from those before 1989. In general, they ask more questions, which is very good. They are more ambitious and self-confident, but sometimes too self-confident.

Katalin Federmayer, 54, Hungary

Federmayer has been teaching since 1977.

It's in the last year of secondary school that we teach the most political material, the 20th century. I graduated from university and started to work in 1977. I knew that what the textbooks of those times were saying wasn't true, but I have to admit that we had very little information at all about events. My parents told me about the 1956 revolution, but I couldn't read about it anywhere. I knew only snapshots. All I could do was to try to make the kids sense which expressions in the textbook were too strong and imposed by the state—like "opportunistic" for the revolutionaries—and show them where information was incomplete. It was a so-called parody of styles. Some of them understood it, others didn't.

I also used different methods. When I was teaching about the French Revolution, for example, I didn't ask the children to learn dates or names but asked them to write revolutionary leaflets and talked about how to organize a revolution. I was never punished for any of this, not even unofficially, though once I did this even when an inspector was in my class. But usually if I closed the door of the classroom, I was alone and did whatever I wanted. I think the kids enjoyed it a lot.

It was an awkward situation. I felt really bad throughout this period because I couldn't do my job properly, though I knew that it wasn't my fault but that of the situation.

In the 1980s things changed a little, because we started to have more and more information about the [1956] revolution from the media. Textbooks started to look even more ridiculous than before. I tried to tell the children everything I knew, but when I asked them later, to check their knowledge, they told me just what they could have read in the textbook. I still don't know whether they did this because they didn't understand what I told them, whether they were scared, or if it was just the easier thing to do for them.

After the transition we had more and more information, but the textbooks became even worse. All political parties printed their own textbooks with their own agenda; it was very hard to remain politically neutral in the classroom. I had to rely on my own conscience and knowledge again. I got a scholarship to go to France in 1994, and I practically spent those four months in the library, reading about things that were published only much later in Hungary.

The problem of textbooks was solved in the second half of the 1990s, when the government regulated the market and set up guidelines for textbooks. Now they're required to be politically neutral, and the basic differences between them are methodological.

Teaching methods and the attitudes of children have also changed a lot. Today a teacher's primary task is not to give information to the pupils but to teach them how to process the information they have. Moreover, it's the children, not politics, that cause the most concern today. After the transition the unequal relationship between the all-powerful teacher and the pupils had to be changed. But today they don't respect the age and experience of the teacher anymore, and I think that this has gone too far.

Dorota Ochal, 62, Poland

Ochal was in the first line of activists who organized opposition groups in Warsaw schools in the late 1970s. She is now retired.

In my teaching, I didn't embrace the new times all that immediately after the June elections and the Mazowiecki government [Tadeusz Mazowiecki, a non-communist, became prime minister after the June 1989 elections]. That was because I had been teaching my pupils what the official history books kept quiet about long before 1989.

Much depended on who the principal was. I used to work under principals who were active members of the Communist Party, as well as those who were not, but I had the luck that they were decent people. And in the mid- to late-1980s, the schools weren't as controlled by the regime as before.

Of course, the atmosphere of 1989 and after was so much different. Before 1989, I had to take care that my lesson plans were in line with the official curriculum, while I'd speak about forbidden topics to pupils. Come the new times, I'd still [speak about those topics], but there was now a record of that, in the register book and in pupils' notebooks.

I used to tell my pupils about the events in Polish history that the regime presented in a completely corrupt way, or didn't present them in any way at all. Now it seems funny, but somehow I didn't talk about Solidarity much and all the then-current events that turned out to be historic. Sometimes you don't see it when history is being made.

But the fundamental change in my job wasn't even that I could teach openly what I had only been able to speak about unofficially before. It was that history ceased to have the taste of a forbidden fruit. It became just another lesson. It may sound strange from a history teacher, but I think that's good. Things returned to their proper order.

Viorel Irimia, 53, Romania

Irimia teaches at two high schools. From 2001 until 2005 he sat on the National History Commission, which adopts curricula.

Before 1989, the aims of teaching history were strongly connected with implementing Marxist education.

One example: history as a subject, as reconstituting the past, was presented according to socio-economic establishments—the primitive commune establishment, the slave establishment, the capitalist and socialist establishments. History was a reflection of class struggle, between those exploiting and those exploited, a transposition, from this point of view, of Marx and Engels' writings.

Clearly, the biggest win after 1990 was depoliticizing the education system. This has been achieved gradually, although history teachers have had difficulty in letting go of old-school language. This was so deeply ingrained in their system that years later some teachers would involuntarily use terms such as primitive commune or capitalist and socialist establishments, etc.

Immediately after the revolution, it was obvious that communist textbooks had to be abandoned. The teaching syllabus was the same. For a few months, teachers were left without textbooks.

For Romanian history, both for 8th and 12th grades, they introduced a textbook dating back from before World War II. This was completely out-of-date and had certain mistakes, scientifically speaking.

Afterward, starting with 1990, new standard textbooks were written, approved, and introduced: 11th grade—ancient and medieval Romanian history, 12th grade—modern and contemporary history. Back then, Romanian history was taught over two years. These textbooks had valuable information, but they carried the disadvantage of offering too many details. They were almost like university compendiums. I once counted more than 200 dates given in one lesson. They also failed to mention certain historical facts and notions.

Gradually, afterward, alternative textbooks were introduced. Not all teachers agreed with [them]—especially in history, because the idea was that history had to be unique, therefore textbooks had to be unique. This [approach] was another Marxist-type throwback. Ultimately, you cannot pretend that you know all truth in history. Ultimately, history is an inventory of certain opinions on certain historic processes and events. From this point of view, alternative textbooks have the chance to particularize history. Alternative textbooks offer you the chance to make the lesson very creative and help students develop skills.

Each history department analyzes all alternative textbooks. Teachers have complete freedom to choose one or the other. Ideally we would also bring students along in this process—except that the textbook selection is made during summer vacation, and it's more difficult to gather the students. ... Ideally the choice would be made together—teachers, students, parents. Probably this is how it will be in the future.

Textbooks and school syllabuses from before 1989 reflected a certain way in which society was organized. Back then, the industrial age was in full swing in Romania. ... Today, we're in a post-industrial era. So today we no longer stress the importance of the quantity of information—even if these textbooks are still rather loaded, and shouldn't be so. Today we stress the building of skills, values, and aptitudes that history can reflect. Skills are what matter—that [students] think critically, relate to other students, be able to interact with children of their age from other countries, peacefully resolve conflicts. … These are values and aptitudes that history can impart.

The first difficulty was to get my hands on all of [the alternative textbooks]. One example: there are seven different 12th-grade [history] textbooks, which are all required in the entrance exam at the police academy. It took me two years to collect them all, because not all publishing houses sent all textbooks to all high schools. …

The second difficulty I had was to develop a catalogue of sources I could use in class. Which means a teacher has to read continuously and become informed. Many themes from before '89 were abandoned, while many others are now included—some of which we didn't even study in college, [for example] migrations in the contemporary age. We never used to talk about that before, other than just a side subject—for instance in World War I or World War II, when people had to migrate. Migrations are also determined by cataclysms. But migrations are an essential topic—for example, how many labor migrants we have today in Western Europe.

So we never studied this in college. In order to be able to teach it, you have to learn it first yourself. This was practically a second university, for those who respected themselves. We had to learn again as if we would have to take exams again—this time the examiners were the students.

I don't miss anything from before 1989. However, I have respect for those times, because they shaped us. And our teachers, our excellent scholars, even if they lived in those times, they taught us well. I have a great respect for my professors in Iasi—without whom, even under those circumstances, we would not have become accomplished as human beings.[4]

Even if the regime was the way it was, valuable people will always be at the top. The regime may have seen things a certain way, but that didn't prevent us from doing our job correctly.

What I regret is that I am no longer as young and no longer have the resilience as back then. I do tell my students that I wish I was that age with today's advantages—from the research point of view. In order to read a specialized book back in the day, you had to go though countless filters and receive numerous approvals … not to mention the [books being] completely forbidden.

Dana Modrovicova, 54, Slovakia

Modrovicova has taught history at public vocational schools in western Slovakia since 1978.

The situation in education has changed dramatically in the past 20 years. Before the Velvet Revolution, history classes strictly followed syllabi. The teacher had no great space to interfere, adjust, or improvise. The program had to be broken down along a precise time line. Classes were controlled by peer teachers and inspections. The school program was fairly politicized with respect to the current regime.

Today, we can teach history much more freely; around 30 percent of the program can be adjusted depending on students' interest. Regarding the freedom from ideology, for example, the lectures on the [1944 anti-Nazi] Slovak National Uprising had to exclusively stress the Communist Party, as if it had been the only one to organize the uprising and as if civil resistance had not even existed. Today, the uprising is interpreted more objectively, civil resistance is included. The teacher-principal relationship has improved. The principal does not represent such an authority anymore, relationships are more collegial. Before, a principal could be only a member of the party and from this position he was also the authority on how to teach.

On one hand, it is good that education has been humanized. On the other hand, the teacher-student relationship has changed—and not always for the benefit of the education process. Teachers' authority has considerably weakened. Teachers' overall social status, including social recognition and financial appreciation, is worse. That has affected students' attitude toward school and teachers. Students are more impressed by people in more lucrative jobs. The previous regime needed teachers more to serve its interests and needs. Teachers' pay back then was above the national average; today it is far below average. Teachers don't drive nice cars and don't wear designer clothes, which young people notice.

Rhetorically, education is still appreciated, but the reality is different. Before elections, the shortcomings of the education system are regularly criticized to rally teachers' votes. But afterward, a lot of it is forgotten.

[The lack of funding] is mirrored in the quality of education—not solely in rewarding of teachers, but also in the school equipment. The job is unattractive for young people, which is a pity, because the new generation brings new energy. Today's education system is mostly an older generation that has failed to figure out how else to make money. We had a lot of young people who loved the job, but they quit to go into business for financial reasons.

The constant turnover in teaching staffs impacts teaching quality. ... In addition, people who teach do various other things for financial reasons. For example, my younger colleagues who feed their families have small businesses—economists do accounting, someone else has a video-rental shop, gives PC courses. Then they are not fully devoted to their vocation.

I'm definitely glad I experienced regime change, which I thought I would never experience. Until then I taught regime change only as a theory from textbooks.

Transitions Online, 16 October 2009

II. POST-CONFLICT LESSONS

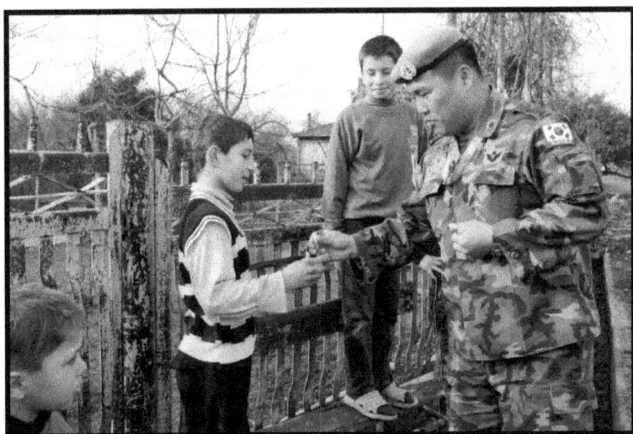

CULTIVATING A MARTIAL SPIRIT

By Tamar Kikacheishvili

*In the wake of war, Georgia adds "military patriotism"
to the curriculum.*

TBILISI

In mid-January, Nona Mikiashvili found out that her 11-year-old son, Lasha, would begin studying something the authorities are calling military patriotism when he returns to school in the fall.

Lasha was excited at the prospect that he might get to handle a weapon, but his mother had doubts. "I don't object to a military course if it includes emergency situations, but it should never be mandatory for all students," she said. "As for patriotism, it's impossible to teach at school. I'm really curious how they're going to teach it. What will they do? Telling students that we [Georgians] are the best, only to have them find out differently later in life, it might cause problems."

Lasha also does not know what to expect from the new lessons in patriotism. He understands that a patriot loves his country, he said. But "Can someone teach you how to love?" he wondered.

President Mikheil Saakashvili's announcement about mandatory military patriotism courses in public schools came about a year and a half after the August 2008 war between Georgia and Russia. Presidential spokeswoman Manana Manjgaladze said military-patriotic education, part of a package of proposals by Saakashvili and Education Minister Dimitry Shashkin, would include training in civil defense and cultivating a martial spirit, "which historically was always in the nature of the Georgian people."

Modernizing an Old Idea

Natia Jokhadze, director of the National Curriculum and Assessment Center, said military patriotism classes would be taught at every grade level and would include civic participation, civil defense, and emergency situations.

The announcement of the course has raised fears about the possible militarization of the country's schools and questions about how patriotism will be defined.

David Zurabishvili, one of the leaders of the nonparliamentary opposition Republican Party of Georgia, said the inclusion of civil defense is simply to give a pretty shape to an ugly idea. "The president announced it, and now the Ministry of Education is trying to figure out how to soft-pedal it to our society. This initiative amounts to militarization, and the idea that everyone must be a militant is the wrong approach," Zurabishvili said.

Saakashvili was not the first to broach the idea of patriotism classes. In November, Irakli Aladashvili, editor of the military magazine *Arsenali*, said military education should be taught in public schools. "I think that the upbringing of the motherland's defenders should start at the school desk," Aladashvili said, calling for classes in civil defense, first aid, and, optionally, weaponry.

In light of Georgia's recent experience with military conflicts in South Ossetia and Abkhazia, Aladashvili said citizens should be able to defend themselves. "We shouldn't be compared with other countries that never experienced war. We had wars within the country as well as in the Caucasus region. I covered the war in Chechnya as well. And I think that Georgian students should study military patriotism," Aladashvili said.

In the Soviet era students were given military lessons, and some countries in the Commonwealth of Independent States still have the subject in their curricula. The textbook for Soviet-era classes typically included praise for the Communist Party and its ideology. Aladashvili said it would be key that the new classes should not be used to indoctrinate students. "I think politics should not have any place in this modern military patriotism course. It should just be about patriotic souls."

Patriotism Without Militarism?

Confused parents are not the only ones uneasy about the new courses.

Some opposition politicians say it's a distraction from Tbilisi's bungling confrontation with Russia. "The Georgian government wants to replace people's disappointment with a sense of patriotism. They're just trying to cover up their mistakes and the pain of a lost war with this new initiative," said Guguli Magradze, leader of the Women's Party, a member of the opposition Alliance for Georgia.

Better to offer peace education in schools given Georgia's recent history, Magradze said. "Peace is the only thing that would give Georgia a chance to take its normal place on the geopolitical map of the world, she said."

More perniciously, Magradze said, the authorities are hoping to cultivate a more pliable citizenry with such courses. "This subject is in the interests of the ruling party, for the purposes of having obedient citizens who obey the dictates of authority. They want slaves. This idea should cause protest in our society," she said.

Tamar Chabashvili, principal of a secondary school in central Tbilisi, disagrees.

Calling the new courses "extremely necessary," Chabashvili said the project would help bring up a new generation of patriots and active citizens. "I think that this subject should include the history and present of the country, including the battles that Georgia had in Abkhazia and the war that happened last year in South Ossetia. It must be a mandatory subject," she said.

Pavle Tvaliashvili, a consultant on education management and reform at the private Center for Training and Consultancy in Tbilisi, said a course that teaches students how to behave in emergencies would be welcome. Nor would he have a problem with a course that aims to instill patriotism.

"I think that patriotism should be used to teach the important values of mankind such as peace, responsibility, freedom, love. … In my opinion, it's wrong to kill others. However, sometimes when someone attacks you, you must be ready to defend yourself," Tvaliashvili said.

Psychologist Gaga Nizharadze, who has written extensively about post-Soviet culture and behavior, said he fears the courses could fuel an increase in violence or bullying among students. Nizharadze said patriotism cannot be taught in a classroom. "Patriotism is not a subject, it's a personal characteristic and that's why it's impossible to have separate lessons in it and to teach it this way," he said.

Nizharadze said the decision to give elementary school students military courses suggests that the country's priority has become militarization.

"Actually I'm against teaching patriotism or any other ideology at school. The only ideology in a democratic country should be that all ideologies are equal," Nizharadze said.

Transitions Online, 16 March 2010

EDUCATION IN A WAR ZONE

By Maysam Najafizada

Afghanistan struggles to implement critical education reforms in a time of conflict and uncertainty.

MAZAR-E-SHARIF, AFGHANISTAN

Seven-year-old Maryam's mother found a black stain on her shirt one day after school. Though the little girl initially denied that anything had happened to her, she eventually explained that, when she was caught outside after a 10-minute recess, the headmaster hit her with his strap as she was running back to class, leaving the mark on her shoulder.

Corporal punishment is still the norm in many Afghan schools, but that is only one of the many obstacles facing education reform in war-torn Afghanistan, where the Taliban insurgency presents an ongoing threat to the implementation and sustainability of the government's policies.

The government under President Hamid Karzai has made progress in education, building new schools and launching teacher-training initiatives. In this "Year of Education Capacity Building," the Ministry of Education has set several ambitious goals, including the establishment of 1,750 new primary schools, as well as the renovation of 962 primary and 475 secondary schools and the development of special schools for disabled children. It also aims to improve the quality of Afghan education by employing around 1,500 school supervisors and establishing a network of school councils that will serve as a conduit for reforms costing more than $15.2 million.

But public enthusiasm for the state's nascent reforms is dampened by several challenges: the persistence of traditional methods for teaching and maintaining discipline in the classroom; teacher shortages and low salaries; obsolete and ideologically charged curricula; and daily physical threats to the safety of Afghan teachers and students.

In some Afghan schools, students are frequently hit with sticks and straps if they disobey, disagree with, or ask tough questions of their teachers. "It's normal. We are used to it. Not only the headmasters but many other teachers use sticks and straps in order to lead students to classes or line them up to listen to the headmaster's speeches," says 17-year-old Ahmad Reshad, who attends a prestigious high school in the northern city of Mazar-e-Sharif.

Some would argue that Maryam, the little girl who was hit by her teacher, is lucky to suffer the strap over the fate of many other female children her age, who are being sold by their impoverished parents, exchanged as settlements in blood feuds between warring tribes and families, or married off at an extremely young age according to tradition.

These practices are behind the alarming statistic that only 13 percent of Afghan girls complete primary school compared to 32 percent of boys, according to the United Nations Girls' Education Initiative in Afghanistan. The disparity is even worse in terms of basic literacy. Only 18 percent of young women aged 15 to 24 are literate, compared to 50 percent of young men in the same age bracket. The general insecurity of wartime Afghanistan, poverty, and child marriage all account for serious discrepancies in female educational opportunities, according to a report by the Afghanistan Independent Human Rights Commission.

Uneducated Teachers

Since the Taliban regime was toppled in late 2001, as many as 6 million boys and girls have enrolled in Afghan schools. However, the supply of students has far exceeded the pool of qualified teachers, and shortages remain a problem even in big cities like the capital Kabul, Mazar-e-Sharif, Herat in the west, and Nangarhar in the east. Afghan teachers are stretched well beyond their capacity.

"Most of our teachers are not versed in modern teaching methods," laments Ghulam Dastager, a professor in Balkh University's Pedagogy Faculty. "They only have knowledge about a subject, not the knowledge of how to transfer it."

That is hardly surprising since many educators are scarcely qualified as professional teachers. According to statistics provided by the Ministry of Education, 80 percent of the country's 165,000 teachers have achieved only the equivalent of a high school education or did not complete their post-secondary studies.

But education officials are confident this situation will soon improve. "Teachers' capacity building is the chief target of the education ministry this year," says Deputy Education Minister Mohammad Sediq Patman. He says that the ministry has launched short-term training seminars for thousands of teachers across the country.

One of the major contributing factors behind teachers' low capacity and morale are their meager salaries, which have not been increased over the last six years.

Fariba, a 35-year-old teacher in Kabul, says, "We can't relax because we don't have enough money to support our families. How can I manage my family with $50 a month? Will it pay for the rent, food, gas, water, or clothes? It's not enough for any of them."

Teachers' basic monthly salaries have been stable at the equivalent of $35 since the current government took over in 2002. In 2008, parliament approved a new budget for the Education Ministry that called for teachers' salaries to be raised to $60 per month. But that hardly provides for a decent standard of living. To give a practical example, the price of a 200-gram loaf of bread is set at an average of $1 by the various municipalities, yet it may be sold at a much higher price in reality. Even with a $60 salary, the most educators can afford is two loaves a day, far from enough to feed both themselves and their families. Many end up taking second jobs to make ends meet, or take bribes from their students in exchange for higher grades.

For many years, officials promised teachers that they would be provided with plots of land to build their own homes, but a series of education ministers have failed to deliver on that pledge.

Khalilollah Hushman, a 42-year-old teacher at Habibia High School in Kabul, recently participated in a teachers' strike over the issue of salary increases and plots of land. "We have the right to strike for a living," he said angrily. "I need shelter for my sons. I need bread for them. The government has paid the least attention to teachers, while we do the most important task in society."

Since the beginning of the Civil War in 1978, school curricula have changed many times under various governing parties. Curricula under the Taliban (and the earlier Mujahideen) were loaded with extremist

Islamic teachings. Even before that, the curriculum was politicized by the communist regime in the 1980s.

The new Afghan government assembled a team of Afghan and international experts to design a new curriculum for primary schools. Plans are also underway to create a two-year curriculum at the preschool level.

"It is a big achievement that the curriculum of our primary schools is being overhauled and our children will be trained well and fairly with the new books," said the ex-Minister of Education Mohammad Hanif Atmar at a ministry press conference when he announced the newly printed books in June 2008.

However, there remains no standard curriculum for Afghanistan's secondary schools and high school textbooks remain woefully inadequate in number and in content. "The books are full of spelling and grammar mistakes and lots of scientific errors in chemistry, biology, and physics," said 18-year-old Ahmad Elias of Bakhter High School in Mazar-e-Sharif.

Schools Without Buildings

"Students who have the opportunity to think about the problems in their textbooks are fortunate," says Dastager at the Balkh Pedagogy Faculty. "They sit on chairs, with desks in front of them and a blackboard or whiteboard in their classroom, with teachers instructing them. We have many students in Afghanistan who don't have the opportunity to think about the mistakes inside their books. They only dream of a building for their school, a chair to sit on, and a desk to write on."

Lack of education infrastructure is a major problem. Hundreds of students are being educated in UNICEF-funded temporary shelters, both in the summer heat and the cold of winter.

Around 4,500 schools are being built, according to a recent government report; however, at present only 40 percent of schools are in permanent buildings. The rest hold classes in the UNICEF shelters or are so-called desert schools with students and teachers gathering in the open.

Some children have to travel great distances to receive a basic education. "I walk 45 minutes to school every day. It is very far for my little sister to go," says 15-year-old Zainab, who lives in Faizabad, provincial capital of Badakhshan.

Under a new infrastructure development program, schools will be built between adjacent villages so that students have less of a commute, said Deputy Education Minister Patman.

In addition to accessibility issues, Afghanistan's political insecurity has threatened all fields of development and the education sector is no exception. The Taliban regularly publish "night letters," unsigned leaflets secretly distributed overnight in the southern and eastern provinces, demanding that parents stop sending their children to government-run schools.

Insurgents also have targeted teachers who have violated their warnings to stop teaching in these schools and, in the far remote villages of the south, have personally appeared in schools, warning that they would kill students that continued to attend.

Says Dastager, "These schools outside the villages can easily become a target for insurgents."

TOL Chalkboard, 19 December 2008

WHEN BULLIES BECOME HEROES

By Andrea Gregory

*Teachers in Serbia are confronting the violent behavior of students
who were small children during wartime.*

BELGRADE

Aleksandar Grandic knows all the best spots for an after-school fight.
Most of the time, he said, kids meet up in tunnels or in the woods.

A Belgrade high school student, Grandic said most fights are organized
to take place off his school's campus, but he recalls regular fights in middle
school that happened on school property, sometimes even as teachers
looked on. He said violence is part of teenage life, especially for football
hooligans like he used to be.

"There are some people who think violence is fun so they beat up
other teenagers," said Grandic, 18, who admits to having been in a few
scraps himself. "Our country is poor. Because of that people drink and
fight. I think in Serbia it's always been like this."

Perhaps, but one humanitarian group is working to make sure it doesn't
stay that way. The Helsinki Committee for Human Rights in Belgrade
will introduce a pilot program to high schools in eight municipalities this
spring designed to help combat discrimination and violence. It will train
teachers in how to deal with such problems and raise student awareness of
alternative ways to react, as well as try to get students to be more accepting
of one another's differences.

"Violence has become a priority of the government," said Sonja
Biserko, head of the Helsinki Committee. "It has become a key word. It's a
big topic here, how you proceed with this violence."

Referring to the country's recent wartime past, Biserko said the troubled children are products of their environment. "They grew up with this model of violence," she said. "It is a horrible situation."

Ivan Kuzminovic, the committee's executive director, concurred. "Criminals became heroes when they were actually killers, not just for children but the whole society," he said. "They are rich, successful, good-looking. Those sort of people simply became role models."

Kuzminovic cited a toxic mix of war, bad role models, and Serbia's postwar isolation, as well as football-inspired nationalism, that is contributing to violent and disruptive behavior in the schools.

According to Kuzminovic, 85 percent of students in their final year of elementary school in Serbia report being victims of violence by their peers.

"It was like that 10 years ago, and it's the same today," he said.

Police officers began patrolling some schools four or five years ago, he said, but the problem persists. He cited the January 2010 beating death of a 15-year-old outside a nightclub in the eastern town of Bor as an example of the extremes such violence can reach.

"The violence is only now becoming visible," he said.

Kuzminovic said teachers can be the victims as well. The most notorious incident happened last year when a 61-year-old chemistry teacher was beaten by a student. The teacher did not report the incident, and it became public only when the attack was broadcast on YouTube, Kuzminovic said.

Tinde Kovacs-Cerovic, state secretary of the Ministry of Education, agreed that this pervasive violence has its roots in the recent past. "Already during the 1990s, there was a clear concern that this kind of atmosphere would have a dangerous spillover effect," she said. "This is not a new phenomenon. It is not something that wasn't predicted."

Kovacs-Cerovic said an anti-discrimination law that the Serbian parliament adopted in 2009 should serve as a beginning to dealing with the problem. She said principals and teachers need to be more accountable for the behavior of their charges and that a violence prevention team should be set up in every school.

Kovacs-Cerovic said programs to counter violence and discrimination tend to be in elementary schools, and funding constraints have kept them from expanding significantly. Only 10 percent, or 120, of the country's elementary schools have programs aimed at stopping violence and discrimination.

Natasa Tucev's 11-year-old son has been on the receiving end of that behavior. She said since he openly declared himself an atheist, other kids in this overwhelmingly Christian Orthodox nation have harassed him. At his previous school, he often had to run away from his classmates, she said, adding that he once hid out in a shop while bullies searched for him.

"The boys form a group like a gang in the class," Tucev said. "They meet him as a group. They attack him as a group."

The Tucev family moved before the start of this school year. Her son attends a different school, and things seem better. But Tucev said she thinks a Serbian mentality helps breed violence in the schools.

"Patriarchal culture is inherently violent because there is the ideal of a warrior hero with a gun or a sword," she said. "Even the kids who were too small for war grew up in that time."

'A Little Society'

Kovacs-Cerovic said teachers need to recognize that they are doing more than lecturing and testing their students.

"Teachers are not just teachers. That is an issue we are now dealing with," she said.

She said the first reaction of most educators is to deny that the problems of violence and discrimination exist. "First everybody says, 'There is nothing.' They don't recognize it," she said. "The baseline is ignorance."

Milena Zivotic is a young teacher in her third year in Serbia's school system. When she started teaching high school math, she thought that would be her sole job, she said. She quickly learned otherwise.

"I want to teach math and nothing else, but I can't because I'm in these kids' lives," she said. "If you're a teacher, you have to create the atmosphere. You have to make connections. School is a little society."

Zivotic said students are looking for adults to guide them. When she surveyed her own students about what they liked and what they wanted to be different, she was surprised by the number who wanted her to be tougher on behavioral issues.

"They want me to control them. Maybe because they're still children," Zivotic said. "These kids are not punished, but maybe they actually want that."

Prime Targets

The few programs in place, and the pilot championed by the Helsinki Committee, would target discrimination as well as violence. To that end, it will include schools with a high population of Romani students, who are consistently the most marginalized in school systems across Central and Eastern Europe.

Many Romani students end up in special education, whether they need it or not. Kovacs-Cerovic said Serbian schools recently eliminated screening before primary school so that entry cannot be determined along ethnic lines. But she acknowledged that many teachers have low expectations for Romani students, many of whom do not finish elementary school. They are just waiting for them to drop out, she said. She said nothing is taught about the history of Roma even though there are some 500,000 Roma living in Serbia.

Still, Kovacs-Cerovic sees some improvement. She said the number of Roma in secondary schools has increased tenfold in the past five years, from 60 to 600.

Some students say they do not see discrimination against Roma, at least among their friends.

Grandic denied that his schoolmates discriminate, except against homosexuals.

"If someone is a gay person in our school, he will get beaten every day," he said.

For some students, change, if it comes, will be too late.

One 18-year-old student in his final year of high school said he has suffered harassment and violence because he is gay.

The student, whose name is being withheld for his protection, said one school beating landed him in the hospital for two weeks. He said he was hit on the back of the head and then fell to the floor. His attacker continued to kick and punch him while he was on the ground. Other students watched, but no one intervened. He said his attacker had graduated the year before and returned to school to seek him out. He dropped the charges against his attacker out of fear of retaliation.

The student said he has heard adults talk about programs to curtail violence and discrimination but doubts that they will make any difference.

"Not in this land because of society, culture," he said. "I don't think it will get better in 10 years. I think it will get worse. I feel helpless and hopeless. I think it will never stop here in Serbia. They don't accept differences here."

Transitions Online, 18 March 2010

JUMPING OFF
A SINKING SHIP

By Hamid Toursunov

*Kyrgyzstan's native-language schools are dying of neglect, while its
Russian schools face a crush of new students.*

BISHKEK AND OSH, KYRGYZSTAN

Among the things Kurmanbek Bakiev left behind when he fled
Kyrgyzstan, alongside an angry populace and empty state coffers, was an
education system starved of investment and expertise.[5]

Once buoyed by the Soviet emphasis on education, the country's
schools now turn out students who score abysmally on international
assessments.

Experts say this education catastrophe is largely a result of an
authoritarian regime uninterested in the abilities of its citizens.

In the meantime, desperate parents have been moving their children
from declining Kyrgyz- and Uzbek-language schools to slightly better-
equipped Russian ones. As a result, demand for Russian-language education
has grown so much that schools can barely cope.

"My parents want me to go to a Russian school," said Guljamal
Sagynaly-Kyzy, a tall, thin 11th-grader at a Bishkek secondary school.
"They say that studying at a Russian school will help me in the future. I
don't know what they mean. Time will tell."

Natalya Charishdalidi, director of curriculum development at
Sagnyaly-Kyzy's school, said that although most of the school's children are
ethnic Kyrgyz, there was not enough demand this year for classes taught
in the Kyrgyz language. "In our school, there are 877 students, and ethnic
Russians are the minority, but we teach in Russian," she said.

Local experts say a similar situation prevails in the south, where about
22,000 Russians live, compared with about 400,000 in northern Kyrgyzstan.

This country of 5.4 million also has a large Uzbek minority, who make up about 14 percent of the population. Russians make up about 12 percent.

"There is a definite trend where the number of children at Russian schools is increasing," said Raisa Toibolotova, director of primary and secondary education in the Education Ministry. "There are many overcrowded schools. Every year, 5,000 to 6,000 children start attending Russian schools."

In 2006, 1.1 million children attended school in Kyrgyzstan, according to state statistics. About 63 percent of students are taught in the Kyrgyz language, 24 percent in Russian, and 13 percent in Uzbek, according to the Education Ministry.

Toibolotova said that even many children who attend Kyrgyz primary schools switch to Russian secondary schools when the time comes. She said textbooks in Kyrgyz often did not make the grade.

"We're a young country, and I wouldn't say our textbooks are bad, but we're still not satisfied with their quality," Toibolotova said.

Toibolotova said parents send their children to Russian schools with an eye to their someday living, working, or studying in Russia. Official and unofficial statistics suggest that nearly all emigrants from Kyrgyzstan head to Russia, with a smaller percentage going to neighboring Kazakhstan.

But Gulchekhra Saidova, a 30-year-old teacher and ethnic Uzbek from Osh, the country's southern capital, says migration is not the key issue. "The main reason why parents take their children to Russian schools is that they offer a better education than Uzbek and Kyrgyz schools," said Saidova, who sends her daughter to a Russian school.

According to the UN's 2009 progress report on the Millennium Development Goals in Kyrgyzstan, "secondary schools face serious difficulties in delivering educational services of appropriate quality."

"Since Kyrgyzstan obtained independence after the collapse of the Soviet Union in 1991, the quality of services provided by secondary schools has been declining," said Munojat Tashbaeva, a sociologist in southern Kyrgyzstan. "The situation is most alarming at Uzbek- and Kyrgyz-language schools. Services are better at Russian schools, which attract more and more parents seeking better education for their children."

The overall competence of students, according to the Education

Ministry, is low. In 2005, 45 percent could not pass a nationwide literacy test and 41 percent failed the test in mathematics.

Intentional Neglect?

In the country's education development strategy for 2007 to 2010, education officials linked the declining achievement to a shortage of quality teachers, textbooks, manuals, and teaching materials, insufficient funding, and poor management.

"The quality of education in Kyrgyzstan is declining," said Duishon Shamatov, an international education researcher at the University of Central Asia. He cited results of the 2006 Program for International Student Assessment, a triennial project of the Organization for Economic Cooperation and Development that measures 15-year-olds' reading, math, and science skills. In its first time participating, Kyrgyzstan scored last in all three areas among the 57 countries surveyed.

These are the fruits of intentional neglect, some critics of the former administration say. In 1990, as part of the Soviet Union, the country spent 7.6 percent of its GDP on education, compared with 4.7 percent in 2005, according to the Education Ministry. In 2007 the figure had edged up to nearly 5.3 percent, according to UNESCO, although a member of parliament recently put it lower in an interview with a local press agency.

Only 39.4 percent of Kyrgyz schools have textbooks, Guljigit Sooronkulov, director of textbook development for the Education Ministry, said in an interview with local media last year.

For the last several years, Kyrgyzstan has been short of 3,000 to 3,600 teachers, for which Bakiev blamed low salaries. The profession has been unable to attract young people in significant numbers: 65 percent of teachers in Kyrgyzstan are older than 45, and 11 percent are over 60.

"The interest of the ruling elite of this country in the quality of education is directly connected with the level of democracy and authoritarianism of the regime," said Alexander Knyazev, director of the Bishkek branch of the CIS Institute think tank and a history professor at Kyrgyz-Russian Slavic University. "If the regime is democratic and wants its people to be socially and publicly active, it tries to give them a good education."

Likewise, Jyldyz Aknazarova, an economics professor and an expert on international education at Osh State University, said: "The poor quality of education in this country leads to a degradation of the society and destabilization of the economy as well as the democratic sector. Economic and social progress takes a good education."

In February 2009, a parliamentary committee acknowledged that improving education must be a priority for the country.

Running Out of Room

Amid this dismal picture, students from Russian-language schools did better than those from Kyrgyz- and Uzbek-language schools on the national test for university entrants for 2009. The growing appeal of Russian schools, however, has created problems of its own.

Alexander Yazov, principal of the prestigious Russian-language Olympus secondary school in Osh, said the demand for places there is so great that he often admits more students than the public school can accommodate.

"In every class, we have about five to eight children more than we should. For example, we should have approximately 30 children in one class. In reality we have 35 to 38 pupils," the principal said. "We don't have enough teachers, and most of our teachers … are over 50. Young people don't want to work at schools. They say salaries are too low," Yazov said, although he added that about 40 percent of students there consistently get above-average to excellent grades.

"There are about 10 elite [Russian] schools in the capital where everything is fine," said Vitaliy Skrinnik, the first secretary at the Russian Embassy in Bishkek. "[Elsewhere] there is a lack of teachers, and I know one village where the Russian language is taught by the physical education teacher, who doesn't speak Russian well, or even Kyrgyz. What can he teach children?"

The teacher shortage mirrors a lack of textbooks. "Though annually Russia provides 40,000 to 70,000 textbooks for Russian schools, only 60 percent of the schools have enough," Skrinnik said.

Charishdalidi, the Russian-language school curriculum specialist, said her school has taken to copying textbooks. "Textbooks published in Russia are expensive, and the [Kyrgyz] authorities don't allocate enough money for books."

Transitions Online, 11 May 2010

THE CANVAS SCHOOLHOUSE

By Bakyt Ibraimov and Talant Sadykov

Their schools destroyed in ethnic unrest, hundreds of Uzbek children in southern Kyrgyzstan will be forced to study in tents.

OSH, KYRGYZSTAN

Violence in southern Kyrgyzstan has left hundreds of children from the Uzbek community without schools.[6]

Mobs burned two public schools in Osh, and an apparent attempt to burn down a school in Jalalabad was unsuccessful.

That leaves some children, like Akbar Mamatov, to live and study in tents, having lost their homes as well.

"We were told that we'll study in these tents for a few months until they build a new school for us since we don't have a school anymore," said Mamatov, one of about 650 students, all ethnic Uzbek, from the Leo Tolstoy school. Uzbek-language public schools are more numerous than Kyrgyz-language schools in Osh, the largest city in southern Kyrgyzstan.

Mamatov, a 13-year-old with eyes that seem older, said, "I went to visit my grandmother before the events, and when I came back home some time later, our school wasn't there anymore.

"Everything was burned down, including our library, so we lost all our books and textbooks."

Still, Mamatov's classmates were luckier than their counterparts at the Hamza school, named for Hamza Hakimzade Niyazi, an Uzbek revolutionary from the early 20th century who had organized free schools for poor children. Authorities say those students will be sent to other schools in the city.

The old site for the Hamza school is too small for a playground and other modern facilities, say teachers at the school and a source in the city's Education Department, all of whom asked to remain anonymous.

In the meantime, Kyrgyz authorities and international donors have set up a settlement of 11 tents on the outskirts of the city, where Osh experiences its own version of urban sprawl.

The area has no infrastructure, and a dirt road connects the tent school with the nearest Uzbek neighborhood, where the Tolstoy school once stood.

One tent serves as the teachers' lounge and a kitchen, but as the school still lacks electricity, no hot drinks or food are available. Students complain of the cold mornings in the tents and say it is uncomfortable, especially when it rains.

Nevertheless, teachers here seem determined to limit the disruption to their students' lives, despite the ethnic tension that is still very much alive in Osh.

"We're doing our best to make our children feel like they're at any other normal school," said Yulduz Alimova, an Uzbek language and literature teacher. "The city authorities said the new school will be built by December, and we'll move in sometime in January."

Alimova and her colleagues say most students are doing well and that they have generally overcome the post-violence stress and have adapted to the new conditions.

"Compared with the pre-conflict time, my students' performance hasn't changed much," Alimova said. "But of course, a tent school can't be compared to a real warm and comfortable school made of bricks."

A shortage of tents forces the school to offer classes in shifts. On a recent school day one tent had been divided into two so that two lessons could be taught simultaneously.

Textbooks are also in short supply. "Before the [violence], we lacked school textbooks anyway, but now in a class of about 20 pupils we have only five or six," said an eighth-grade student, who introduced himself as Aibek. "Those who have books do their homework. Others just attend classes, but they don't get bad grades because our teachers go easy on them because of the difficult conditions we have now."

But there are currents of optimism here.

"In general, we're doing OK. Of 843 schoolchildren [who attended last year], about 658 attend our school, and this is a big success for us, when lots of people are still fleeing the city," said Murodullo Muidinov, the principal. He said the new school will probably not be built before winter sets in, so winterized tents and heaters will be installed.

"Of course, we realize the quality of the teaching we provide under such circumstances is quite low, and our schoolchildren aren't learning properly," one teacher said. "But the main thing now is to keep our teaching staff working and have the new building constructed so that children of our community in this part of the city don't lose their school."

Ethnic Exodus

Other schools face a converse problem, as they remain standing but are losing their students. Although reliable statistics are not available, schools teaching in the Uzbek language in Osh seem to have lost as many as half of their students, and ethnic Uzbeks continue to leave the country.

"This year I took my daughter to the first grade for the first time, and there was only one class, compared with four last year where my neighbors' children study," said Khakim R., an Uzbek taxi driver, who asked that his full name not be used.

School administrators complain that local authorities prohibit them from releasing the real number of pupils attending schools.

In the city of Osh, 55 of 57 schools are open — 21 of them teaching in the Uzbek language, 14 in Kyrgyz and nine in Russian-language, with the remaining schools teaching in a mix of languages.

"The children who don't attend school anymore have simply gone to Russia with their parents or are kept home because their parents are afraid to let them out," said I.A., the vice principal of an Osh school, who asked for anonymity. "Last year, we had about 1,100 schoolchildren, and this year only about 600 showed up."

For their part, education officials downplay the number of missing pupils. According to Abdybaly Boltobaev, the head of the city education department, 93 percent of school-age children are attending school, the independent AKIpress agency reported.

But that figure is impossible to verify, and other evidence suggests that the government figure is inflated. Azattyk, the Kyrgyz service of Radio

Liberty, reported that this year only 41,000 children are attending school in Osh, down 18 percent from 50,000 last year.

"Nobody can say for sure either the real number of children attending schools or the number of people who have the left the country since June 2010," I.A. said. "Ethnic Uzbeks leave mostly for Russia and other countries; as for the Kyrgyz, they leave for Bishkek."

Isa Omurkulov, the acting mayor of Bishkek, said his city's schools are overcrowded, with a need for 30,000 more seats, according to AKIpress.

Meanwhile, Akbar Mamatov attends the Tolstoy tent school every day, rain or shine, despite the long walk he takes to get there.

"It takes me about 30 minutes to walk to the tent school, and the road isn't paved, so it's either muddy or dusty depending on the weather," said Mamatov, who walks with a limp. "I don't want to miss my classes because my peers will laugh at me, saying I'm weak and can't walk long enough to reach our school."

Transitions Online, 12 October 2010

ON THE WAY BACK?

By *Athar Parvaiz and Animesh Roul*

Optimism that the educational system in Kashmir has started to recover from years of conflict has been tempered by recent events.

SRINAGAR AND NEW DEHLI

In May of this year, four Kashmiri candidates passed India's prestigious civil service examination. But what sparked celebration all across the region was the rare feat achieved by one of them, Shah Faisal, who topped the examination with the best score. This was the first time that as many as four Kashmiri youth had qualified for India's civil service—and that one of them excelled above all others was the icing on the cake.

The results in the civil service test, one of India's most competitive exams, led to almost a month of celebrations. Faisal was driven to his native village with a fleet of cars. "It was an outburst of pent-up emotions as Kashmiris have witnessed nothing worthwhile happening in the last 21 years, particularly in the field of education," said psychologist Malik Roshan Ara.

The students' success was the latest sign that the education system in Kashmir has at last started to recover since the devastation wrought by the latest conflict over the disputed territory, which started in 1989 and quickly accelerated over the following years before abating in 2004.

During years of intense conflict in the Indian state of Jammu and Kashmir, which claimed tens of thousands of victims, the education sector suffered the worst fate next to tourism. By 1995, a four-member committee from New Delhi, headed by the social policy analyst Joseph Gathia, concluded that children were the "biggest victims of violence in Kashmir."

The Gathia committee found that more than 400 schools were gutted during the early 1990s; more than 60 percent of children between the ages of 10 and 14 were deprived of educational opportunities because of the surrounding violence; paramilitary forces occupied a large number of rural school buildings; and the presence of those soldiers in and around educational institutions created a psychosis of fear among school-going children.

The academic atmosphere in the entire Kashmir valley atrophied because of the physical turmoil and psychological pressure of conflict. The abrupt large-scale migration of Pandits (Kashmiri Hindus) from the valley due to the armed conflict meant that the system lost many of its teachers.

Disruptions in the academic calendar were brought about by violent incidents and repeated strikes, not to mention dereliction of duty by education staff claiming that they were avoiding the conflict. Education standards were not enforced, leading to rampant plagiarism and several cases of brazen cheating on standardized examinations.

Teachers on the Run

It would be hard to overestimate the impact of the Pandit exodus. Until the beginning of the conflict, members of Kashmir's Pandit community had filled most of the vital positions in every sector, including education. Those in the teaching profession had usually commanded respect from the Muslim community owing to their zeal, commitment, dedication, and high standards of learning.

"The schools in earlier times used to be mainly manned by the Kashmiri Hindu teachers, given the fact that most of the educated people belonged to the Pandit community," said Raza Ali, a senior teacher in a government school in the frontier Kupwara district. "But right after their migration to Jammu and other areas, a sudden dearth of teachers led to further crises apart from the fallout of violent incidents and a fear psychosis."

According to the available statistics of the education offices of several different districts in the Kashmir valley, more than 1,100 Kashmiri Pandit teachers migrated from the valley.

Initially, the migration also had an impact on the educational prospects of the children of the Pandit families who had left, many of whom found it difficult to enroll in new schools. The problem was especially acute in Jammu, an administrative region within the state of Jammu and Kashmir. According to Abdul Gani Madhosh, a retired professor and noted educational expert, local authorities opposed the idea of putting the new arrivals in the same classrooms with their peers, evidently fearful of generating competition for the locals.

"Due to some specifically local reasons, the Jammu administration did not permit Pandit children to mix with Dogras [the majority local ethnic group] in various schools so the Pandit children had to be kept separately," Madhosh wrote in his 1996 study *Children Under Armed Conflict in Kashmir—The Educational Scenario.*

The initial resentment from the Dogras of Jammu ultimately faded away. "One apparent reason for this acceptance of non-locals by Dogras was that they finally came to terms with the fact that the presence of Kashmiris could hardly jeopardize their prospects in their own land," said Ara, the psychologist. "They were also impressed by the hardworking attitude and capability of Kashmiri Pandit students."

This change of heart allowed the Kashmiri Pandit students to continue their studies in a peaceful atmosphere in Jammu, and strive toward academic excellence.

Meanwhile, their counterparts back in the Kashmir valley continued to suffer because of the raging conflict. Not surprisingly, the abnormal security situation in Kashmir left a lasting impact on the performance of Kashmir-based students. While the Jammu-based students—including Kashmiri Pandit students who had migrated to Jammu—fared better in exams and evolved into qualified professionals and technocrats, the Kashmir-based students saw their prospects decline due to a lack of proper infrastructure, instructors, and more importantly, unfavorable learning conditions under constant violence.

According to Bashmir Ahmad Dar, a former director of academics for the Board of Education in Jammu and Kashmir, students then at middle- and secondary-school levels, as well as those graduates studying for their bachelor's degrees, were particularly affected during the initial decade of turmoil in the valley. "[They] are the worst hit since it had become next to impossible to hold classes and fair examinations in those years," he said.

That reality is well illustrated in a comparative analysis that Madhosh undertook of the pass percentage of Jammu-based students and Kashmir-based students.[7] From 1990 to 1994, Jammu-based students obtained an average 60 percent pass percentage while the students in Kashmir produced only an under-40 pass percentage. Students who had migrated elsewhere, to Delhi and other states, were able to put up even more impressive numbers than those in Jammu.

According to Madhosh, the situation in the education sphere in Kashmir has started improving with the decrease in violent incidents. "We can say that our students now feel relaxed and free of the psychological burden so as to think of participating in, and clearing [passing] high-level competitions," he said.

"Though we still need to go a long way, we should feel encouraged by the latest trends," Madhosh added. "Kashmiri boys and girls have now started applying for international scholarships, a phenomenon which was missing when the conflict was at its peak."

"Exams are no longer interrupted by day-in and day-out strikes, and female education is on the increase," Madhosh continued. The improvements, he said, are not because conflict-related incidents have stopped occurring. "But thankfully the education sector is now the least-hit sector, just the opposite of what it used to be during the 18 years of conflict."

Such progress has been achieved despite the decision of Pandit teachers not to return. But over the last 10 to 12 years, many Kashmiri youth have secured higher degrees from universities in Kashmir and abroad, and a large enough number have decided to become teachers to start to replenish the teaching ranks.

But education infrastructure is another matter. Even though most of the school buildings damaged during the conflict have been rebuilt, conditions in some places remain horrendous. Some classes are still held in open fields and temporary shelters. One of the schools in the southern hamlet of Nagbal was found to be operating from a cowshed while another north of Srinagar was located in a storefront. According to a recent study by Kashmir's Department of Education, more than 50 percent of schools have no drinking water facilities, and 60 percent schools lack toilets. Playing fields are available only in 7 to 10 percent of schools. And in many places there are not enough seats for students.

Worries Return

The last few months have placed a damper on Kashmiris' optimism. Renewed protest demonstrations, strike calls, and repeated scenes involving young boys throwing stones at security forces (as a mark of protest against the presence of Indian forces in Kashmir) are a fresh threat to the education system and led to school closures across the valley.

Since June 2010 more than 60 people have been killed during anti-India protest rallies, including young people shot dead by Indian security personnel. Buoyed by public support, several political parties have launched a "quit Kashmir" movement asking India to give up its claim on Kashmir. They have said that strikes and protests will continue until India leaves.

Teachers find themselves caught in the middle. The Indian government requires school teachers to ensure attendance even during strikes or they may be faced with dismissal, but observers say that the current situation throws up serious obstacles to obeying that order.

"During strike calls, restrictions on the movement of people are also imposed by the government in an effort to stave off protest demonstrations," explained Dar, the former state education official. "And then there is also the problem of the non-availability of public transport during strikes and curfew restrictions."

After remaining shut for 100 days, schools in Kashmir Valley reopened on 27 September 2010 with students and teachers given free passage by security forces despite a curfew and restrictions in many areas.

However, attendance was thin against the backdrop of Kashmir separatist leader Syed Ali Shah Geelani's call to parents not to send their children to schools and colleges.

TOL Chalkboard, 5 October 2010

PRESSURE
STARTS YOUNG

By Vishaka Wehella

Children in Sri Lanka face intense competition to do well at a young age, but that's far from the only problem in an educational system racked by inequality.

COLOMBO

Shamindra Jayasinghe is a grade four student at Subharathi Junior School in Godagama, near the Sri Lankan capital Colombo. One day, he came home from school scarred and shaken. His father, Mahendra, confronted the boy's teacher, who admitted to beating Shamindra and kicking him out of the classroom for not bringing his Tamil-language textbook that day to school.

No matter that the class schedule for that day included no Tamil-language lesson, and Shamindra was not the only one to have left the book at home. His gumption at being the only student to try and explain his "mistake" had apparently prompted the violent reaction.

But the family believed there was also another reason for the incident. The teacher had been conducting paid private classes for students of grades three, four, and five. Two-thirds of the students from Shamindra's class attended those private lessons, but he was not one of them, earning the teacher's ire, according to the boy's parents.

This case highlights the problems that can happen when a student dares to question the teacher in the rigid Sri Lankan education system that favors rote memorization over inquisitive thinking. And it also showed how highly competitive exams, starting at a very young age, have transformed the system into one that favors those who can afford to pay extra tuition for special private classes.

As in Shamindra's school, children throughout the country begin preparing in the early years of primary school for their first competitive barrier: the Grade Five Scholarship Exam. Two separate exams test mathematics, language skills, and general knowledge. The students with the highest marks receive the opportunity to enter popular and prestigious schools in the cities.

The system was launched in the 1960s with the intention of awarding scholarships to rural students from poor family backgrounds. However, the market economy that was introduced in the late 1970s has drastically transformed the nature of the scholarship exam. Besides spawning a thriving market for various practice tests, the changes have led to the emergence of tuition-based private classes as practically an obligation for students, or at least those that can afford them. They must start young or risk getting left behind because of the huge competition to enter the better schools in Sri Lanka.

For example, every evening, the streets of the Colombo suburb of Nugegoda are flooded with students on their way to and home from private classes—from young pupils in grade six to high schoolers studying to get into university. The majority of those who attend these classes in cities close to Colombo are students of the better schools in the capital. Tuition fees vary between 2,000 and 5,000 rupees ($17-$43) per month, quite a lot of money in a country where the average monthly household income is 35,500 rupees ($319) and one-quarter of people live in poverty. Those studying for the Advanced Level (A/L) examination, the competitive test for university entrance, usually attend many classes, at a cost at least 6,000 rupees per month.

Teachers conduct most of these private classes after school and during weekends. The examination results clearly show that urban and semi-urban, middle-class children receive higher marks on the exams and enter popular schools. Poorer children, whose parents don't have the money for private classes, are at an obvious disadvantage and only very rarely do well enough to best the fierce competition.

Champa Dahanayaka is a teacher from a well-known girl's school in Colombo, among those that usually produce the best results on the A/L examination. She is very critical of the current teaching style.

"Our results are 100 percent. OK, but sometimes I ask myself whether we properly teach our students or just train them to run a race," Dahanayaka says. "From the day we start the Advanced Level, we teach them how to answer the question papers [the practice tests]. What we are doing is, instead of providing knowledge, just teaching them how best to answer the questions on the examination."

The result of this highly competitive examination system is that students who memorize well and reproduce the right answers at the examination will advance, but those who have the capacity to critically analyze but might not be the best at rote memorization will be rejected.

Unequal Resources

Although the Sri Lankan Constitution states that all Sri Lankan children have a right to a proper education, experts say that the categorization of schools has made that constitutional right a farce. With the intention of allocating resources equitably, the authorities select a single school in each divisional secretariat, or administrative area, and provide those schools with basic physical resources, such as computer rooms, sports equipment, and perhaps financial support for upkeep and maintenance.

Yet huge discrepancies among those schools is evident. For starters, since all the popular schools are located in the center of cities, and the main qualification for admission is permanent residence close to those schools, mainly the children of the urban elite fill these coveted places.

That reality has accelerated the emergence of a network of private schools in urban and suburban neighborhoods. Such schools have been a relief to parents who either didn't want to send their children to government-run schools or whose children had failed to gain acceptance for one reason or another.

Although growing numbers of students study in private schools in Sri Lanka, those schools do not come under direct supervision of the Ministry of Education; instead, these schools are simply registered with the Board of Investment, which oversees the country's commercial sector. Many question whether such regulation is sufficient.

"My eldest daughter is in grade six now. I was really delighted with what she gathered from the school in her primary grades, especially as she was taught in English," says Wiranthi Mallika. "But now my daughter frequently complains that her science teacher makes mistakes in English while teaching. So I am puzzled as to whether these teachers are competent enough to teach in English."

Falling Behind in English

Educational reforms in the 1940s called for free education for all Sri Lankan children and a system that did not place a premium on English-language instruction. Since then, many things have changed. Recent trends have indicated that English-language knowledge is key to getting a good job, yet many students are graduating without that ability. Reforms in 1998 tried to remedy the problem through the introduction of English in grades one through five and English-language instruction for grades five through nine for subjects such as mathematics, science, social studies, and environmental studies.

Today, however, the plans to overhaul the use of English in schools have largely failed. Even the popular schools merely have English as a separate class instead of teaching many subjects in English. A report released in 2008, 10 years after the reforms to boost English-language instruction, found a decline in the quality of the teaching of subjects in English as a result of the lack of trained and skilled teachers. The report recommended a five-year-long, in-service training scheme to increase the number of qualified personnel.

Inequality in the distribution of English teachers among schools is also a problem. Although the government has failed to recruit English teachers to schools in the so-called plantation sector (where the students are predominantly children of Indian laborers), in some urban schools, there are so many English teachers that some have been appointed to teach other subjects.

"Our children have been educated in Sinhala for nearly 40 to 50 years," says Sucharitha Gamlath, a veteran teacher who has been campaigning for an English-language education system in Sri Lanka. "So it is difficult to transfer the education medium from Sinhala to English overnight. Initially we will require a pool of qualified teachers who will need to undergo full-time training in English."

A Paucity of Teachers

There is a shortage of qualified teachers in other subjects as well. In 1994, the government presented a "Teacher Service Enactment" after considering the ideas and proposals of working professionals, education specialists, and teachers' trade unions. The enactment included new recruitment schemes, proper procedures for awarding promotions and granting transfers, and new salary scales. But similarly with many other programs in Sri Lanka, government inefficiencies have translated into a lack of the support services needed to implement such reforms and live up to their grand ambitions.

In the meantime, teachers' unions have complained that the government still does not have a proper recruitment policy designed to maintain the quality of education.

Every teacher in Sri Lanka who graduates from university must first work in a remote area for four years, a compulsory requirement. These are often very tough assignments where the infrastructure and resources of the schools are minimal, and, with fewer teachers on staff, the workload is heavier.

Pubudu Siriwardhana is a teacher who was appointed to one of these remote schools in the Southern Province. "The total number of students in my school is 75, and there are five teachers," he says. "Among them, three are graduates and two are education diploma holders. But our principal has neither qualification."

Yet with the unpopularity of these rural postings, qualified people are hard to come by.

Critics of the country's education system also wonder why the fairly large allocation from the annual budget (8 to 10 percent)—not to mention the expenses incurred by parents for private tuition classes—continues to yield such overall poor results.

In 2008, of those students who took the Ordinary Level (O/L) examination—as opposed to the advanced level one—49 percent failed in mathematics, 68 percent in English, and 55 percent in science.

Experts see a variety of reasons behind such disappointing figures, such as unqualified teachers and the emphasis on rote memorization instead of analytical thinking. Over the years the conflict involving the Tamil Tiger insurgency also meant that some rural schools might not have had sufficient textbooks or other resources to educate their students.

"The results of the O/L examination were not at a satisfactory level," said Thilokasundari Kariyawasam, an education specialist. "Those who are in the education sector, including the respective ministers and school principals, should take responsibility for this failure. If this situation is not improved immediately it will, no doubt, get worse."

TOL Chalkboard, 19 May 2010

III. THE
PRIVILEGED CLASS

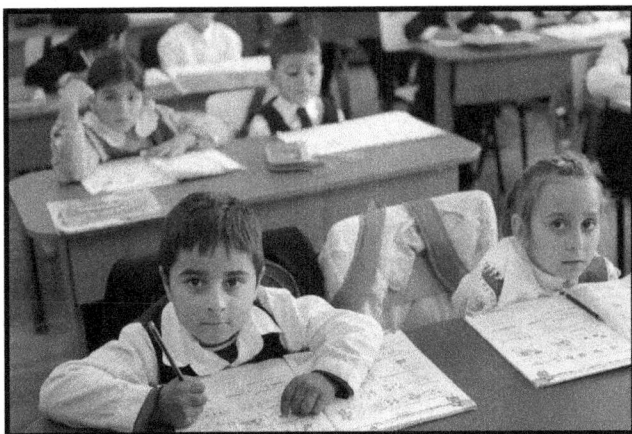

A TERRIBLE THING TO WASTE

By Galina Stolyarova

Education in Russia is becoming simply
another tool of the ruling party.

ST. PETERSBURG

It was an amicable-seeming offer that the academic felt was impossible to resist. So the rector of a state-funded technical university in St. Petersburg, who also holds a senior position on the city's council of rectors, agreed to join the pro-Kremlin United Russia party.

No threats were made, but the scholar knew that denying such an offer would get him blacklisted immediately. It was all very informal. A group of senior members of the local branch of the party approached him, suggesting that it was perhaps unwise for an academic manager of his rank to distance himself from the party endorsed by the president.

"He is a professional, he has a team, and he is trusted by the team," one of the rector's colleagues said in his defense, sounding both frustrated and apologetic. "The most important thing at the moment is that the school provides the students with a good degree, and if the price to pay for that is the head holding a party ticket, well, he decided he can live with it."

This story about Russia's most powerful party recruiting a new member would appear unremarkable under other circumstances, but it helps to reveal the pattern of politics interfering on various levels in the country's education system.

For starters, being a rector in modern Russia has become a political post in the Soviet tradition, when the country's ideological gurus kept the education process under strict control.

Lyudmila Verbitskaya, who had been rector of St. Petersburg State University for 15 years until she stepped down this month to become the university's first honorary president, has campaigned vigorously for a third term for President Vladimir Putin.

She also served as a "steamer" in the regional list of United Russia during elections to the St. Petersburg Legislative Assembly in March 2007. In Russian political jargon, a steamer is a prominent person who agrees to appear on a party list and be used to draw voters to the polls for the duration of the election, like a railway engine drawing carriages and then retiring to the sidings.

Verbitskaya's previous initiatives included a proposal to close the popular but defunct political puppet show *Kukly* on the nationwide NTV channel for "creating a distorted and insulting image of President Putin."

Class is Canceled

But, of course, there is much more to this issue than the position of rector becoming a politically charged post.

Two major educational organizations funded by foreign sponsorship and grants have come under fire from the Russian authorities in recent months on what critics see as far-fetched technicalities with an ulterior motive.

Lectures at the European University in St. Petersburg were suspended when the city's fire inspectors found 52 violations. The district court twice ruled against granting the university permission to hold classes while correcting the violations. Most suspicious is the fact that although the fire inspectors' complaints were directed against the building that houses the university, the court's ruling affected the teaching process itself.

The judgment orders a "temporary suspension of activities," which makes it impossible for the university's management to rent out other premises until the argument over the historic premises has been resolved.

The phrasing used in the verdict carries a strong whiff of political pressure.

Liberal politicians and human rights advocates have referred to what they see as a possible connection between the closure and a recent conflict over an educational project that involved independent monitoring of elections in Russia and informing the Russian people about the electoral process.

The project, funded with a 673,000-euro grant from the European Union, had drawn criticism from a United Russia member of the State Duma, who called for an inquiry into the university's activities and for the project to be suspended.

On 30 January, the university's Scientific Council voted to shut down the project on the grounds that "part of the activities involved in the project does not correspond to the school's license."

Worryingly, the university's rector, Nikolai Vakhtin, declined to be more specific when confronted with requests from reporters to give a more detailed explanation behind the decision.

One False Move

"For friends—everything; for enemies—the law." This formula, devised by the late Spanish dictator Francisco Franco, provides a key to understanding Russia's current strategy for applying legislation. In other words, justice in Russia is highly selective.

Private companies in Russia long ago learned to read the warning signs that they have somehow displeased the authorities.

For instance, receiving a visit from both the fire inspectors and the tax police in the space of a month gives a clear hint to a company that it is on a dangerous collision course with the authorities. If a health and safety team then arrives, the company's bosses know they are in deep trouble—and not because of their suspect company accounts, faulty firefighting equipment, or dirty kitchen.

Some of the fire "violations" at the university would take several years to correct. Because it is in a historic building protected by the state, any changes to either its exterior or interior would require lengthy coordination with a number of state organizations. For example, the university was asked to remove a narrow 19th-century spiral staircase. To do that, the school's management would need the approval of City Hall's Committee for the Preservation and Protection of Historical Monuments—which of course may never be granted.

The university's management found itself at a loss over such complaints because the staircase has always been there and did not present a problem on any previous annual fire inspection.

Over the course of the last two months, the European University has been subjected to two other inspections investigating the legitimacy of its registration and operations, and even the content of its courses.

Unlike the British Council, which, after a direct confrontation with the Russian authorities, was forced to close down its branches in St. Petersburg and Yekaterinburg, the management of the European University has tried to use the same weapon that had been used against it.

After two lost cases, it became clear to its managers that neither logic nor perseverance in correcting the listed violations was working. So Vakhtin made a careful but powerful political statement. He pointed out that the university was founded by the late St. Petersburg mayor, lawyer Anatoly Sobchak—the man who brought to politics and is revered by both Putin and his protege candidate in the forthcoming elections, Dmitry Medvedev.

Vakhtin took matters further by stressing that the campaign against the university clashed dramatically with Medvedev's praise of the university as an innovator—the European University was the first academic institution in the country to implement an endowment scheme for its funding—as well as the politician's relentless calls to cut down on red tape in education.

The Science and Higher Education Commission of the St. Petersburg government has since suspended the university's license. No clarifications or comments have yet been made.

The Bad Old '90s

In the wake of the closures of the British Council and the European University, Viktor Sadovnichy, rector of the prestigious state-run Moscow State University and another prominent "steamer" of the United Russia party, gave a revealing interview to the political weekly *Itogi* in which he expressed frustration over the many private universities and academies in Russia that emerged in the 1990s as a result of liberalized legislation.

"I have the feeling that education remains some kind of an experimental polygon. ... In the Soviet Union there were 600 universities, but now there are 3,345 non-state ones alone," Sadovnichy complained. "We are still reaping the consequences of the policies of the 1990s when three people could gather in the kitchen and declare that they had founded a university."

Indeed, there were fewer universities in the USSR, and the state had a firm, unrelenting grip over all the schools that existed. In the Soviet Union it was unthinkable for a high school graduate to get a place at a university—no matter how brilliant his or her grades—without being a member of the Komsomol.

Similarly, being excluded from the Komsomol could have meant immediate expulsion from university and certainly would have put an end to any serious career, be it in international relations, Russian literature, organic chemistry, or theoretical physics.

Unlike many academics at state universities, professors from the European University don't participate in political activities. The school is not a remotely dissident organization. Its mission is to produce not only qualified professionals in social and humanitarian sciences, the school's core areas, but also responsible citizens capable of critical thinking.

That was the goal of the electoral project that the school was forced to shut down. But the Russian authorities seek to impose strict control over people's minds rather than nurture independent thinking.

Put simply, the state wants to regain its grip and incorporate the education system into its vertical of power. Perhaps the rector of the European University will soon be invited to join United Russia.

Transitions Online, 28 February 2008

NO MORE TEACHERS, NO MORE BOOKS

By Farrukh Akhrorov

Tajikistan wants to teach Islam to its children, in its own way. But critics say the effort is hobbled by paranoia and corruption.

DUSHANBE

When Nozigul Khasanova learned that courses in Islam were going to be introduced in Tajikistan's secondary schools, she welcomed the news.

Khasanova, who lives in the west near Dushanbe, said she had always wanted her 16-year-old son to know about the religion and that a course taught in public schools could help "keep children away from various radical groups."

But the roll-out has been a disappointment. "The school's physical education teacher occasionally gives lessons [on Islam]," she said. "He was picked because he goes to the mosque and has read several booklets on Islam."

Education officials' ambitious plans have fallen into the gap between intentions and reality. Authorities blame a shortage of qualified teachers. Others say the pool of instructors would be larger if the schools were willing to employ imams or more people who have studied the Koran in Arab countries.

In the meantime, school children are learning from unqualified instructors and some schools still offer no such courses.

Islamic studies were introduced in line with President Imomali Rahmon's directive to honor Abu Hanifa, an eighth-century imam who enumerated the laws of Sunni Islam. His 1,310th birthday was marked by public festivities in Tajikistan in 2009.

An education official in the southern Khalton region, speaking on condition of anonymity because he feared retaliation from the Education Ministry, said teachers of Islam are required to know the Koran, including its earliest versions. They also must know the difference between *suras*, or chapters of the Koran, and *hadiths*, which depict episodes in the life or the words of Muhammad.

But he said there are few scholars who fit the bill, "and they don't want to work in schools because teachers get paid so little and they would find it immoral to constantly beg students' parents for money."

Learning to Improvise

He said some principals manage to improvise, but "Islam is not yet being taught in most schools." Nor, he said, has a uniform syllabus been developed or textbooks printed. In July 2009, Tajik Education Minister Abdujabbor Rahmonov said a textbook on the subject was in the works and would be released before the end of the following month. Education officials said the textbook has not yet been published "for unknown reasons" and would not comment on the minister's promises.

Rahmonov told a teachers' conference in Dushanbe in August 2009 that schools had as many as 1,440 vacancies. Education officials blame staff shortages on the low salaries of teachers, who are paid about 250 somoni ($50) per month on average, according to the ministry.

The country has about two dozen teacher training schools, and an official with the Khujand University rector's office who spoke on condition of anonymity said more than 800 teachers graduated from that university alone in 2010. Nationwide, the number was about 2,000. He said most were offered jobs at schools in Tajikistan's northern Sogd region, one of the impoverished country's most economically developed areas.

To address teacher shortages, Nurullo Giyasov, dean of Khujand University's Language Faculty, suggested that schools invite in imams, many of whom he said would be willing to teach for free, seeing it as an opportunity to increase their flock. Giyasov said several graduates of his school's Arab language department teach Islam in schools, but he acknowledged that the need is much greater.

But some Tajiks eager to teach the subject say their efforts are blocked by the ministry.

Parviz Radzhabov studied Islam in Yemen but he cannot find a teaching job and temporarily works as a merchant at a food market in Qurgonteppa, a city south of the capital. He applied for jobs at mosques, madrasas, and secondary schools but, he said, "many employers are suspicious of those trained in Arab countries. They view them as terrorists."

The government and media of Tajikistan are controlled by a small group of relatives and associates close to the president. Although some parts of the mountainous country, which borders Afghanistan, are effectively out of Dushanbe's grasp, the authorities keep a watchful eye out for those they consider potential jihadists or Islamists. In the autumn of 2010, government troops were sporadically fighting what the government says are Islamist militants in the central Rasht Valley but what others say are the remnants of the other side in the country's civil war in the mid-1990s.

Radzhabov said he has been trying to conceal his foreign Islamic education lately for fear of "problems that some religious people have, especially those holding degrees from foreign Islamic centers." He said that women wearing hijabs "are not allowed to trade in the neighboring market, while market owners threatened to impose a fine of 100 somoni [about $23] on those wearing religious clothing."

Many of Radzhabov's friends would prefer to study Islam in Tajikistan, he said, but "there are few theological schools in the country, while most young people know nothing about the existing ones." He suggested that Dushanbe's Islamic University and other schools promote their services to attract applicants, "inform [people] about their courses and teachers' qualifications and open branches all over the country. But there is nothing of the kind here. The government bans a lot of things but doesn't offer anything in return—this is one of the sources of possible tensions in society."

In speeches this summer, Rahmon urged Tajiks to persuade their children studying at foreign religious centers to come home to study at Dushanbe's Islamic University or one of the country's dozen theological schools. He also promised that the Committee on Religious Affairs, which oversees religious organizations in Tajikistan, "will send as many youths as our country needs to study at foreign madrasas [that] do not teach various terrorist and extremist doctrines."

Mavlon Mukhtor, deputy chairman of the religious affairs committee, told reporters that of the more than 1,400 students studying at madrasas elsewhere in the Muslim world, about 50 returned home after the president made his appeal.

A Generation of Cynics

A survey conducted last year sheds light on why so few students took up his offer. In mid-2009, a group of Tajik journalists asked about 3,000 high school students and graduates here about their plans for the future. Nagris Muhammadi, a member of the group, said the answers suggested that the country's long-standing and pervasive corruption have disillusioned many young people.

Muhammadi said many young Muslims told the pollsters that they "do not plan to study in Tajikistan's official education establishments or plan to stop attending classes there. They believe that the education system is plagued by nepotism and one cannot study without bribes, whereas Muslims consider [corruption] a sin." Many of those wearing religious clothing do not feel comfortable in Tajikistan "because others pay too much—unhealthy, in their opinion—attention to their clothing and behavior," Muhammadi said. Many of those young people would prefer to study religion on their own or at Islamic centers in the Middle East, he said.

Giyasov, of Khujand University's Language Faculty, noted that countries across Central Asia are struggling with a shortage of Islam teachers and the lack of a religious syllabus suited to contemporary life. He said the solution lies in regional efforts. "There's no need for every country to begin training highly specialized staff like instructors of Islam," Giyasov said.

Meanwhile, students at many schools in Tajikistan do not even know that the new subject exists. Khurshed Iskandarshoyev, an 11th-grader in the town of Khorog, in the southeastern autonomous region of Gorno-Badakhshan, is among them. He said that several years ago he "had classes on the history of different religions, but they probably did not have enough teachers because various teachers, for instance industrial arts, geography, and literature instructors, taught the subject, with big gaps between when the classes were offered."

Transitions Online, 9 November 2010

SCHOOL
FOR SCANDAL

By Onnik Krikorian

Alleged abuse at an Armenian school for the disabled led to a criminal probe—of the young activist who blew the whistle.

YEREVAN

In what is still a conservative and hidebound country, Mariam Sukhudyan hardly comes across as typical. The smell of incense wafts across her family's modest apartment in the Armenian capital, and meditative music plays softly. Her bicycle, a rarity in a car-obsessed culture, takes up most of the hallway that leads to the front door.

But the low-key, even passive figure Sukhudyan cuts at home belies her situation in the unwanted glare of official attention.

Sukhudyan, 29, made her name as an environmentalist, protesting the felling of parts of the vast Teghut forest in northeast Armenia as part of plans to develop a copper mine. But while her counterparts find themselves politically isolated, Sukhudyan faces prosecution for publicizing alleged physical and sexual abuse of students in one of the country's dilapidated, Soviet-era boarding schools for children with physical, mental, and emotional disabilities.

Complaints about conditions at the institutions are nothing new. While enrollment at the schools has declined from 12,000 to 5,000 in recent years, some remain dumping grounds for children from socially vulnerable families, who enroll their children in the schools to get food and clothing sent by donors.

Critics say school directors, who receive funding on a per-capita basis, oppose government plans to return children to their biological parents, or place them in foster care, and integrate them into mainstream education. That plan is backed by international children's organizations such as

UNICEF and World Vision, whose officials argue that a focus on inclusive education is better for many learning-disabled youngsters than effectively hiding them away in residential institutions.

"A strategy is being implemented to restructure boarding schools, but the issue is one of finance and a lack of specialists in this area," said Kristine Mikhailidi, child-protection officer at World Vision Armenia, a nongovernmental organization. "De-institutionalization should occur by 2015, but the situation remains one of concern."

Sukhudyan's claims, however, went well beyond issues of substandard care. After volunteering at the Nubarashen No. 11 boarding school in Yerevan last year, she told local media about conditions there. The main public television station aired her accusations last November.

"According to accounts from the children, they are subjected to beatings and other forms of physical punishment," said an online statement signed by Sukhudyan and 11 other volunteers at the school. "We personally witnessed needlessly harsh treatment of children by teachers and night guards. The school director and other administrative workers use children as a free labor force in their homes and summer houses."

After investigating the allegations, the police brought defamation charges against Sukhudyan, exposing her to up to five years in prison. None of the 11 other volunteers who went public faced prosecution. The charge was changes to slander, but Sukhudyan still faces up to three years in jail and a fine of 100,000 to 500,000 dram ($260 to $1,300).

"The new charge is because of the publicity surrounding my situation, and because they simply can't prove the previous charge," she said. A conviction for slander rather than defamation would also make Sukhudyan eligible for an amnesty introduced in the wake of post-election violence in 2008—but only in exchange for admitting guilt, which she has refused to do.

"I'm innocent," Sukhudyan said. "Why should I lie and say I'm not? I do not want to make my life easier. It's simpler for me to go until the very end and to the European Court of Human Rights if necessary."[8]

The allegations helped prompt Armenia's government to form a committee to monitor the boarding schools. Many familiar with the facilities also take the volunteers' accusations seriously.

"Physical abuse is always there," Mikhailidi said. "They are yelling, they are beating on these kids, and all these things are happening. Closed facilities, no interaction with society, no one is coming in, they don't have skills to work with these kids—all this brings an abusive situation."

'Active Imaginations'

A teacher accused by two schoolchildren of sexually abusing them resigned soon after the allegations were aired, but generally the school's head of education, Donara Hovhanissyan, denied claims of widespread abuse.

Sukhudyan and her colleagues "didn't understand that every child here has mental disabilities and very active imaginations," Hovhanissyan said. "It's very easy for them [the children] to make something up."

Sukhudyan acknowledges she never witnessed any sexual abuse at Nubarashen. But she stands by the children's claims.

"This little girl who was speaking about serious sexual abuse was terribly distressed," Sukhudyan said. "She was in such a state that I was saying we shouldn't ask any more questions because she was in such emotional distress."

One of the departed teacher's two accusers has since retracted her allegations, but Sukhudyan contends she did so under pressure from school officials. She said the teenage girl discussed the matter with another Nubarashen volunteer and that a recording of the conversation was turned over to the authorities, who rejected it as material evidence. According to Armenian press reports, the official transcript of the recording omits any discussion of the alleged coercion.

At a press conference in early November, Sukhudyan's lawyer played the recording and accused the authorities of tampering with evidence. Prosecutors subsequently ordered a fresh investigation of the case, on the grounds that the recording, and the testimony of the other alleged victim, who has not recanted, were not accepted as evidence in the original probe.

Rather than welcome this seeming victory for the defense, however, Sukhudyan said the delay was frustrating, as she was confined to Yerevan pending a resolution of the case, and thus prevented from traveling to public meetings on the Teghut copper mine.

"I can't help but link this case with Teghut, because I'm not the first activist to be subjected to such pressure," she told Radio Free Europe in an August 2009 interview. "This may be a good opportunity [for the authorities] to break our movement and force me to shut up."

Other prominent civil society activists express similar concerns. "It looks like active citizens are not encouraged in our country," Sona Ayvazyan of the Armenian affiliate of Transparency International, told journalists at a demonstration by Sukhudyan's supporters. "The authorities seem to be trying to eliminate such citizens one by one. Mariam is simply the latest victim, and we don't know who will be next."

TOL Chalkboard, 1 December 2009

OF COMPUTERS AND MEN

By Galina Stolyarova
*In which the best-laid plans to stem corruption
in the university admissions process go askew.*

ST. PETERSBURG

Russia has launched a new system of Unified State Examinations for final-year high school students. The three-hour test, evaluated by a computer, largely determines who gets a place at university.

A few weeks after the exams ended, tens of thousands of losers are busy filing appeals with the Education Ministry, while some of the lucky ones are telling the simple secrets of their success. A financial sweetener given to a teacher did the job in one case, while on another occasion it was as easy as agreeing to meet a friend in the toilet at a certain time to share information.

It was not really that Marina, a St. Petersburg high school student, was not confident about her knowledge of history, but she arranged to meet a classmate in the women's restroom during the exam to discuss any tricky parts. The tactic worked, and the two girls, who used their time in the toilet effectively, are now happy university students.

At another school, the parents of the pupils simply collected 35,000 rubles ($1,150) and bribed a teacher, who helped them to obtain the tests beforehand and do a bit of last-minute preparation.

"I got unofficial access to the test at 6 in the morning, which was four hours before the start of the exam," one of the pupils told me.

A teacher has to be present to monitor the exams, but many who passed said that rules are routinely violated. Although mobile phones are banned in the exam room, for instance, some pupils said proctors were turning a blind eye to students sending text messages throughout the process.

Not all pupils were so resourceful. Although nationwide figures are not available, many regions report hundreds or even thousands of protests against the apparently malfunctioning system. Parents who are helping the unfortunate students to prepare appeals face ridiculous restrictions. One family said they were denied the right to even make a copy of the test results.

Testing Began in 2001

The Unified State Examination was proposed in 2000 as a means of fighting corruption. Proponents said an impersonal computer verdict would give a better idea of a pupil's knowledge than the presumably subjective opinion of a teacher. The exam was held in selected regions on an experimental basis in 2001.

The outcome of the latest experiment is disheartening. First, because the move has apparently proved ineffective against corruption. Bloggers across the country relate anecdotes about how the test is taken in some remote village schools, with just a handful of pupils in the room sitting in front of their teacher, who effectively helps them out. Every region in Russia has to report the examination's results to the Education Ministry, and no region wants to look bad.

Some of the regions tried a bit too hard. Irina Shapovalova, the education minister for the north Caucasus region of Karachaevo-Cherkessia, was fired by the region's president, Boris Ebzeyev, for what he described as "abnormally good results" compared with the Russian average.

In addition, many who took the test complain that the procedure of filling it out is confusing and flawed. "For example, in one of the questions, I had to give the title of the famous novel by Mikhail Sholokhov," one student recalled. "I gave the title, *And Quiet Flows the Don*, and then the computer listed my answer as wrong, simply because I wrote the title in quotation marks. Then another answer was counted as wrong because I referred to one literary work as a war drama but should have said it was a patriotic war drama." Several other pupils have complained that the computer did not find their writing legible. Such technicalities now cost students a place at university.

Perhaps a solution is to give the pupils a choice between different types of exams, or at least to give the current system an overhaul. Not only is it a rather feeble way of resisting corruption, the new system appears to deprive students of the chance to show they have an understanding of the subject and focuses instead on a somewhat arbitrary number of facts that have to be presented in a precise way.

As it stands now, the Unified Exam is excelling in turning sense into nonsense.

Transitions Online, 5 August 2010

EVERYBODY GETS A PIECE

By Ruzanna Rashidgizi

Experts fear that Azerbaijan's long-awaited education law does not promote transparency.

BAKU

After nearly 15 years of stalled efforts and heated debates, parliament passed a long-awaited new law on education, finally replacing a 1992 law that had regulated education since the country's independence from the Soviet Union. President Ilham Aliev signed the law into effect on 7 September.

Lauding the initiative of his ministry, Education Minister Misir Mardanov promised that the new law would be effective because "…it meets all modern requirements and corresponds with [Azerbaijan's larger] reforms."

But education experts are not so convinced. Some analysts and teachers have called the new law a step backward, arguing that it adds to the existing lack of transparency in Azerbaijan's education system.

"This new law smells of authoritarianism," said Etibar Aliev, who heads the 21st Century Education Center nongovernmental organization. "It has no liberal values, no democratic principles. We signed the Bologna declaration in 2005, which aims for a more European style of education and, much to my regret, the new law is in contradiction with it."

"We cannot leave behind socialism, and we cannot join developed countries either," said Siyavush Novruzov, a deputy of the ruling New Azerbaijan Party during the first reading of the bill. "See the document and you will understand everybody is trying to take a piece for himself."

The State Commission on Students Admission, known by its Azeri initials as the TQDK, has taken issue with still granting winners of academic

Olympiads admission to universities without having them undergo compulsory standardized exams, despite widespread objections after the first reading of the bill.

All students are supposed to take standardized tests administered by the TQDK, an independent body. Introduced in 1992 and based on the American model of standardized admission tests, the written exams were designed to judge students' aptitude for higher education. According to the new education law, students must continue to take the exams, but a vaguely defined "appropriate executive office" is now charged with deciding where they will be admitted. Exams to obtain masters' degrees are now evaluated by the same office instead of the TQDK.

These vaguely defined offices are a matter of great concern to education experts because no one knows exactly who will handle these responsibilities. "Appropriate executive office" is repeated more than 40 times in the new law.

Rovshan Agayev of the Centre for Economic Initiative Support says that these vague terms will cause big problems "because executive offices make decisions behind closed doors and those decisions are at a higher level than the rule of law." For example, many now fear that state university tuition increases are on their way.

"The heads of schools will do whatever they want, because there's no rule [in the new law] about the fees for universities," said Etibar Aliev.

Such fears are not unwarranted. Tuition in state universities has increased three times since 2003. According to the Centre for Economic Initiative Support, it costs $600-$2,100 per year to attend Baku State University depending on the program, while the average annual cost of study at the State Economic University is $1,600. The average yearly salary in Azerbaijan is around $4,500.

Boost in Education Spending

"In spite of the recession, the Azerbaijani government spent $297.5 million more on education this year," the education minister said during a national teachers conference on 5 September. The government's education budget in 2008 was $1.3 billion.

Meanwhile, the World Bank contributed $25 million toward the strengthening of the Azeri education system over the period 2008 to 2013.

The World Bank money was earmarked for technical improvements, mainly to purchase computers for schools, while the state allocations went toward building new facilities, renovations, textbooks and other resources.

The government says it has built hundreds of new schools and renovated many others, as well as boosted the number of computers in schools from one per 1,032 students in secondary schools to one per 29. The Education Ministry plans to give 400 laptops to its best teachers and students, as determined by Olympiads and academic competitions organized by the ministry. The ministry also plans to build new physics and chemistry laboratories in 100 schools.

"That's a boom," said Bayram Huseynzade, a spokesman for the Education Ministry. "Using these millions, we will try to change not only schools but the content of education at the same time."

But many teachers say this rosy picture doesn't reflect the real situation in schools.

"Nothing has changed for me," said Terane Kandalova, a mathematics teacher at a secondary school in Baku, in response to the government's announced achievements. "Pupils come to school just to get their certificates. They don't even want to answer our questions; good pupils go to tutors. Nobody is interested in teaching them at school. You have to pay tutors if you want your child to be taught."

Kandalova was referring to the common practice of employing external tutors to help students prepare for standardized exams and admission to higher education. While she receives a monthly salary of $80, private tutors can earn up to $200 per month, per pupil.

According to Kandalova, students hardly value the role of teachers in their own education or in society. "Everybody can get a certificate by paying off the director of their school. Teachers are nobodies. And we have to pay the director to pick up more lessons, so we can make higher salaries."

"I'm so tired, as both a parent and a teacher. I feel so terrible, so useless," Kandalova added.

Another teacher at a secondary school in Baku, who asked that her name not be used, was similarly skeptical. "How do you fight it, using the law?" she asked. "Don't raise my blood pressure, please. Our director has his own rules and laws.... I go to [work] just because I don't want to stay at home."

She was also angry because the school that her three-year-old grandson attends recently asked their family to pay a compulsory fee. According to the Education Ministry, all kindergartens in Azerbaijan are provided free of charge. Furthermore, the new law stipulates that every child should go to kindergarten. Many parents say it is hard to secure a place without paying a "fee."

Malahat Murshudlu, head of the Free Teachers Union, thinks increased budget allocations for education are not nearly enough to reverse corruption. "The attitude to education must be changed. There are good and honest teachers, but there are people who see the school or the university as a money pit … and their attitude to education affects the pupils and students around them. There are decrees and orders, but no control or monitoring, and that's the cause of corruption."

The efficacy of increased education expenses was further questioned by the recent results of middle school exams: Scores from 2009 graduates were the worst in five years. Half the students obtained less than 140 points out of a maximum 700 and only 6.5 percent received 500 to 700 points, according to the TQDK.

TQDK Chairwoman Maleyka Abbaszade, says her commission will investigate why many graduates who received high marks upon leaving middle school couldn't reach even 100 points during admission exams to high school.

Every middle school pupil must take an exam upon leaving school. Students who fail the exam do not receive their certificates and are held back for another year. This policy was applied for the first time in Baku in 2008, and took effect nationwide in 2009. "One of the most successful reforms of the Education Ministry this year was middle school leaving exams. We will not give certificates to pupils who do not have the knowledge," Huseynzade said.

Mardanov acknowledges that his ministry still has a great deal of work cut out. Despite the recent changes and budget increases, he says there is a shortage of 7,000 teachers in the rural areas of the country; no foreign languages are being taught in 10 percent of the country's schools; more than 80 percent of schools and universities do not have adequate heating in the winter; and 600 sub-standard buildings are still being used as schools.

TOL Chalkboard, 25 November 2009

THE PHILOSOPHER-KING

By Lena Smirnova

Books by Central Asian leaders are no novelty, but few are as ubiquitous or unavoidable as those of the Uzbek president.

TASHKENT

Here is a pop quiz: Who is the prolific author of the 15 volumes of books and speeches that are required reading for Uzbek students in a course on "The Idea of National Independence: Main Concepts and Principles"? If you said President Islam Karimov, you pass.

Karimov's voluminous writings began to enter the curriculum in many Uzbek schools in the early years after independence from the Soviet Union. "In all, young people [study Karimov's writings] for nearly 10 years, but even university students don't know the president's works in detail," says Farkhad Tolipov, an associate professor of politics at the National University of Uzbekistan.

Tolipov, who like all aspirants for the postgraduate candidate of science degree had to take an examination on Karimov's writings, says students' less-than-enthusiastic reception of the leader's thoughts speaks to their ironic attitude toward official documents and slogans.

"The course is boring and the books are boring," one Tashkent undergraduate says. She passed her course on Karimov's writings in each of her first three years, and this year must take the mandatory exam in the subject.

Writing books and publishing collections are in the tradition of Community Party bosses and socialist leaders, says Uzbek sociologist Bakhodir Musaev, adding: "That is their culture."

Karimov's first book offers an overall prescription for renewing Uzbek society and the political system. Two others cover economic matters, and the fourth and best-known looks at security concerns and offers more guidance on politics and public life.

"There are at least three effective criteria for defining the degree of democracy in a society" that work, Karimov's *Uzbekistan on the Threshold of the 21st Century* states, defining the criteria as "the extent to which the public is informed about decision-making processes, the extent to which governmental decisions are under the control of the public, and the extent to which ordinary citizens take part in state management.

"If there is no progress in these three fields," it continues, "then all discourse about democracy is either mere populism or simply a political game."

Karimov is not alone in writing about politics and his take on the world—regardless of whether it is viewed as political guff, insightful literature, or pure propaganda. The current Kazakh, Tajik and Turkmen leaders are all published authors, and Saparmurat Niyazov, the long-serving first president of Turkmenistan, notoriously required that students read his spiritual guide, the *Ruhnama*, and ordered its display in mosques.

But Karimov's writings have represented the official gospel for years, even if there is disagreement on their merits.

"More than 10 years have passed since these true words were written, but real actions indicate that there are neither guarantees for progress nor any movement," Musaev says.

One retired educator recalls that in the early years of independence, students and teachers embraced the leader's writings.

"In our lessons, we convinced students that national independence would lead to a better life and that life in Uzbekistan would soon improve," the former Tashkent teacher says. "At first students sincerely believed that independent Uzbekistan would become a prosperous, highly developed country, citing Karimov's books. But then they lost interest in the course and in Karimov's books because life in the country hardly improved."

In Soviet times, the woman taught university students the history of the Communist Party of the USSR. Just as students in those times prepared written summaries of the classics of Marxism-Leninism, after independence students who wanted a grade of "excellent" summarized Karimov's books.

When Tolipov defended his dissertation in 1997, he took exams in his specialist field of political science, philosophy, information science, and a foreign language, in addition to the works of Karimov. He passed that test with a good mark, but says that even the university staff who set the exam to postgraduate students did so unwillingly and considered it an unnecessary burden. He calls the exam an anachronism from the Soviet past.

'Insights on the Man'

But not everyone regards the president's books as propaganda or self-aggrandizement. S. Frederick Starr, founder of the Central Asia-Caucasus Institute at Johns Hopkins University's Washington campus, said in an e-mail: "What strikes me above all is his tendency to dwell on problems, or at least on those problems that he perceives, rather than engage in the endless self-congratulation that is natural to the genre."

Starr contributed the preface to the 1998 English-language edition of *Uzbekistan on the Threshold of the 21st Century.*

"I did so because it offered insights on the man, and especially on his tendency to seek to manage all change, a tendency which I traced to the years he spent working for the Soviet planning agency, Gosplan. I characterized him as something of a pessimist, for whom the 'glass is always half empty,' " Starr says.

The book was an "important new work" of "remarkable frankness," Shirin Akiner of London University's School of Oriental and African Studies wrote in a comment for the book jacket.

Karimov has built a reputation as one of the region's harshest rulers. His government often comes under criticism from human rights defenders for its rough measures against those it considers enemies, often members of Islamic organizations. The press is tightly controlled and civil society groups closely monitored. Karimov, who has ruled Uzbekistan since Soviet days, was re-elected in December 2007 to a seven-year term with 88 percent of the vote.

Just as Karimov has come to embody the secular, authoritarian Uzbek state, his writings are taken as expressing the thinking of the entire leadership—whether or not he wrote everything under his name.

Musaev claims the books "are the products of the collective thought" of members of a presidential think tank called the Institute of Strategic and Regional Studies, and influential presidential advisors.

But the poet and journalist Rakhmatjon Kuldashev believes the authorship of the books doesn't matter because they reflect the views of Uzbekistan's leadership.

"The ideology stated in his books, being the ideology of the Uzbek president and government, was necessary to divert the nation's youth away from Islamic fundamentalism in the early 1990s," Kuldashev says. "Young people were affected by Islamic fundamentalism and Karimov's books were aimed against it."

Starr believes that Karimov is the real author of all or at least much of what is in the books, "and that they therefore are in their way revealing."

"I suppose it is not a bad thing that these people [Central Asian leaders] consider it important to write, or have someone write, books, but they always reveal more than is intended," he says.

Numbers Are Deceiving

Despite the relatively low price of about 2.50 euros for a volume of the collected works or 30 cents for a pamphlet of a speech, there is no obvious demand for the Uzbek president's writings. Many Uzbeks seem to prefer books or pamphlets on the teachings of Islam.

Booksellers show respect to the author-president. On entering one bookshop in central Tashkent, the first thing the customer sees is a display of his books in a glass case decorated with a vase of flowers, below the flag of Uzbekistan and Karimov's portrait.

An Uzbek librarian told Radio Free Europe that 31 million copies of Karimov's works had been published, exceeding five-fold the print run of Lenin's writings issued in the republic under communism.

"I am not aware that any of the many books by leaders of the new states of Central Asia have had much real impact," Starr says.

"I suppose it is a not a bad thing that all these presidents feel the need to issue books on economics, history, or ancient history … even if they are little read and have a very brief 'shelf life.' Perhaps they are like the books that political candidates write in the West."

Transitions Online, 2 April 2008

IV. PRIDE
AND PREJUDICE

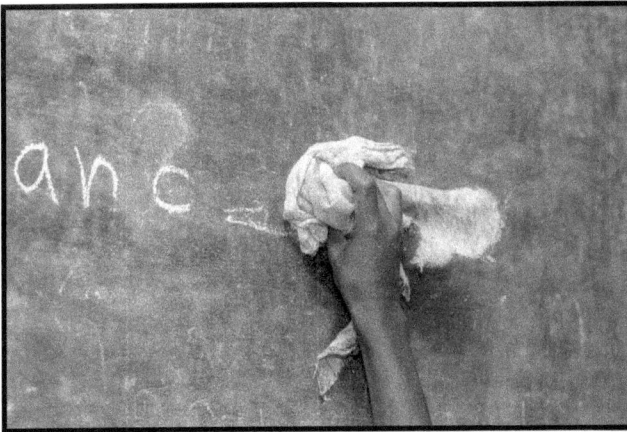

TEACHING DIVERSITY BY THE BOOK

By Sinziana Demian

*A schoolbook becomes popular with a message that the majority is
just one among many cultures living in Romania.*

CLUJ-NAPOCA, ROMANIA

Hamburgers are originally from the northern German city of Hamburg.
Cappuccino was named after the brown-robed Italian Capuchin friars. The
dragon symbolizes wealth, luck, prosperity, and heroism in Chinese culture.
Hebrew is read from right to left. In Hungary people celebrate Mother's
Day and Women's Day separately, unlike Romanians, who meld the two
holidays into one on 8 March.

That's a small sampling of the trivia third- and fourth-graders are
getting to know, thanks to "multicultural" textbooks being used in a few
dozen schools across Romania.

The handsome publication, *Multicultural Education: Third and Fourth
Grade*, is the first of its kind in Romania, and it highlights 23 ethnic groups
who live in the country. Each two-page chapter provides a few basic details,
such as the community's population and location in Romania (marked by
red dots on a map), along with a few words in the community language
from a child's basic vocabulary ("hi," "boy," "girl," "teacher"), a trivia box,
and a little story from the folklore of that particular ethnic group.

"For inspiration, I used several textbooks from schools for immigrants
and minorities in different Western European countries and then adapted
the concept to Romanian conditions," said Simona-Elena Bernat, an
education expert from Cluj who co-authored the book with primary
school teacher Zoltan Molnar.

Break with the Past

Bernat said she paid particular attention to the quiz sections at the end of each lesson, trying to come up with interesting and thought-provoking questions. Students are asked to continue the stories or come up with different endings, interpret certain symbols, and, most importantly, try to apply the lessons learned to a situation in their daily lives. This is a welcome departure from standard textbook drills, which often simply require students to reproduce information found in the text.

The textbook was piloted in 2005 under a joint initiative of the nonprofit Ethnocultural Diversity Resource Center in Cluj and the Belgian King Baudouin Foundation. Twenty primary school teachers received hands-on training in using the book in optional classes with third- and fourth-graders. In Romania a teacher stays with one class throughout the first four grades, so teachers are free to teach the material at their own pace.

The book was published by the diversity resource center with financial support from the central government's Interethnic Relations Department. More counties have quickly begun adopting it and distributing it free to schools. The appeal of the optional classes has become so great that the Education Ministry includes them on its official list of suggested optional courses. Typically, primary-school teachers use this one hour per week for extra math and Romanian language drills.

"When I first received this book, I was slightly skeptical, thinking that an additional subject would just burden the syllabus too much," said Ecaterina Fodorean, a teacher at Nicolae Balcescu School in Cluj. "But then I skimmed through it and felt more confident about it. It's a great opportunity for students to learn facts about other ethnic groups living in Romania. They can use their knowledge from geography and history to understand certain things, such as how and why these people ended up living together with us."

With a mixed class by Romanian standards (one half-Italian pupil, one half-Arabian, and one half-Hungarian student in a class of 26), Fodorean particularly appreciates the interactive features of the book, which allows students to apply personal experience and be creative. She said parents have embraced the class as a means of broadening their children's knowledge of other cultures in a nonjudgmental way. Another teacher, Cristian Arapu of

Avram Iancu School in Bistrita-Nasaud, said the book repeatedly underlines how cultural diversity can enrich children's lives.

More than 2,000 copies of the texts are now in use by students, and the book's popularity is such that teachers are sharing it and making photocopies for their own classes.

Know Your Salad Ingredients

The communities treated in the text range in size from the Ruthenians (numbering 257 in the 2002 census) to the 1.5 million-strong Hungarians; newer arrivals such as Arabs and Chinese are also featured. Apart from various ethnic groups—including the majority Romanians, in keeping with the authors' inclusive method—the book introduces intercultural themes like women's lives, race, and religion. Bernat said the biggest challenge was to avoid stereotypes and to make the book and the exercises equally interesting to children from different backgrounds and locations.

"The general tendency in Romania is to present diversity through conventional elements such as folk costumes and old holiday traditions. I agree that these have enormous significance, but they may not appeal to all children as much, especially to those from an urban environment, who are never exposed to such things in their everyday lives," Bernat said.

If a visual revamping of the old-style texts was not always possible—most pictures in the book present traditional costumes, activities, and settlements—the exercises are more modern. Children are asked to identify the cultural group or groups they belong to and to talk about differences and similarities they have noticed within their own communities, discuss various family values, or explain certain religious symbols and their significance. In another chapter they are challenged to identify real versus imaginary categories from a dialogue among different kinds of fruit all destined to be mixed up in the same salad.

The success and ever-rising demand for the textbook gave rise to the idea in 2007 to produce a multicultural calendar suitable for students of virtually any age. Distributed free to students, the wide-format calendar presents daily factoids pertinent to Romania and abroad: that retired Romanian football star Gheorghe Hagi is of Macedonian descent, that the Olympics allowed women competitors for the first time in 1900, or that the International Red Cross was established in 1864. They also find out about the Armenian genocide, the Romani alphabet, and the national days of neighboring countries. Calendar users also become aware of the various cultural backgrounds of many famous Romanian artists and scientists.

Bernat, who also co-authored the calendar, said it can inspire students and teachers to develop their own projects. "They can collect information from basically any area of interest and produce much more sophisticated calendars themselves," she said.

Transitions Online, 5 November 2008

WINDS OF CHANGE FROM THE NORTH

By *Natalia Lazareva*

A new research institute aims to preserve traditional cultures and develop educational resources for the indigenous people of northern Russia.

KHANTY-MANSIYSK, RUSSIA

When thinking about Russia, almost every foreigner names three geographic entities: Moscow, St. Petersburg and Siberia.

Vast, snow white and bitterly cold, Siberia seems to be deserted in the popular imagination. However, in spite of its low population density, more than 30 ethnic groups inhabit Siberia, including Aleuts, Chukchi, Nenets, Dolgans, Evenks, Selkups, Chuvans, Kets, Khants, and Mansi.

About 30,000 Khants and Mansi live in the autonomous Khanty-Mansi district, one of the most important Russian regions because of its oil and gas industries. Traditionally hunters and anglers, they also engage in cattle rearing and reindeer breeding. Due to the rapid development of Russia's energy industry, the area's population has increased by 1 million people over the past 30 years even as the nation's population has declined. Newcomers to the region have had a strong impact on the unique languages, native cultures, and lifestyles of the indigenous groups.

Irina Nikiforova has been studying the people of Siberia for many years, and is conducting research on the ancient forms of government of the autochthons of the North. "Among the major problems, I am sorry to name the following: depopulation of many groups, alcoholism, loss of national identity and traditions," she said, when asked about the most pressing social problems affecting these people today.

Experts say the problems could be mitigated by the development of better indigenous education services. At present, there are primary schools and various education institutions that teach the basics of national trades and languages, though they are mostly located in remote national settlements and are short of teaching staff. Furthermore, the education of ethnic groups still revolves around the state curriculum, which facilitates the further assimilation of each indigenous generation into Russian culture.

To counteract the decline of national traditions, the Khanty-Mansi district government, together with the Russian Academy of Education, established the Research Institute of Small-Numbered Indigenous Peoples of the North. Its purpose is to unite scientists and researchers interested in preserving the culture of Northern ethnic groups and developing targeted education for them.

The establishment of the institute dovetails with federal government policy on the issue. At the beginning of 2009, Prime Minister Vladimir Putin backed a plan to strengthen protection of indigenous populations of the North and improve their quality of life.

According to L.N. Koveshnikova, acting director of the Khanty-Mansi Department of Science and Education, the main areas of research will be pedagogics, cultural studies, psychology, linguistics, and anthropology.

More Teachers, Textbooks

One of the main expected goals of the Research Institute is the development of language textbooks on the Khants and Mansi languages. Moreover, it is planned to systematize accumulated data on the culture of the various northern ethnic groups and provide public access to this information. The institute will also help to solve the problem of teacher shortages in ethnic schools.

The institute is not without its critics. Irina Nikiforova does not believe that the establishment of such an institution will help native people. "There are already a great number of foundations devoted to the problems of the peoples of the North," she said. "Meanwhile, ethnic groups are losing their national identities rapidly and dying out. It's my own opinion, and I hope it will turn to be false."

Maria Longortova, a student of the Russian State Pedagogical University's Faculty of Peoples of the North, is more optimistic: "I am sure that the creation of this Research Institute is reasonable, as it will help to organize all the information we already possess. I am Khant myself, and understand my native language a bit, but I can't say a word. So I am waiting for the textbook."

TOL Chalkboard, 1 June 2009

INTENSIVE CARE

By Barbara Frye

Making the rounds with health mediators in a Romani village:
birth, death, and everything in-between.

DIOSIG, ROMANIA

Kati Gurbai and Tunde Makai gingerly pick their way through ankle-deep mud until they reach the home of Argentina Kanalas. It's a cold mid-December afternoon, but Kanalas is standing outside, clad in a thin, long-sleeve shirt and full-length skirt.

She has finely arched eyebrows, plum cheeks, pretty brown eyes, and brown hair, pulled back, that falls in wisps around her face. In another place and time, she might be a photographer's or artist's model. Instead, she's a poor 16-year-old, five months pregnant with her second child and afraid to go to the doctor.

"You have to go to the doctor. She needs to see how you are," Makai tells her. "It's for your health, for the baby's health."

Kanalas shyly holds her hands behind her back and protests mildly. "I had the baby at home last time and it was fine," she says. A neighbor, also a teenage girl, interrupts with a tale of her own: she gave birth in a hospital, she says, and when her baby needed an intravenous injection, the nurses put the needle into the baby's head. Now the spot is infected, she says.

It's nothing Gurbai and Makai have not heard before. The two women are health mediators, trained by social workers and medical professionals to reach out to members of this Romani settlement in the town of Diosig, a Hungarian-speaking part of northwest Romania.

Each day, they walk from their houses nearby through this community of 1,500 people. Their rounds can take a day or a few hours. Sometimes they have certain people they want to check on. Other times, the people along the way call them into their yards.

They also sometimes accompany people from the settlement on doctor's visits, which can be a difficult experience for patient and doctor.

Gurbai and Makai, who have been mediators for five years, were chosen after Makai's father, a Rom who sat on the local council, nominated them. Each earns a salary of 150 euros per month.

The women said it took about six months for the Roma here to accept them.

"The first problem when we came was nobody understood what we wanted," Makai says. "They didn't know how to go to the doctor, where to go to the doctor …" she says, her voice trailing off.

"They were afraid. They didn't want to show us their papers or give their real names," Gurbai adds.

The mediator program aims to improve health care in Romani communities by making sure Roma have better access to care, are better educated about their own health, and have smoother interactions with medical professionals. Some Romani communities have Romania's highest rates of tuberculosis, hepatitis, and AIDS, and Roma, who often eat poorly and smoke heavily, face high rates of heart disease and cancer. Romani CRISS, a Bucharest-based advocacy group, started the program in the late 1990s.

A 2006 independent evaluation of the program called mediators "the most important driving force in spreading information and educating the Roma population, as well as in creating the necessary environment for a trust-based relationship between Roma patients and health-service providers."

For Gurbai and Makai, the first task was to make sure the people in the settlement had the required birth certificate and identification card in order to receive health benefits. Then each person had to be assigned a primary doctor and have a medical file created.

The 2006 report estimated that mediators had helped 8,000 Roma enroll on family doctors' lists but that more than 7,300 were still to be registered in communities where mediators worked.

The women are now welcomed into the community, but with each new birth, those basic tasks must be attended to. Kanalas, for instance, lives with her boyfriend's family because her father is out of the picture and her mother has taken Kanalas' first child's birth certificate in order to receive the state benefits that go to poor children, about 70 euros per month. There isn't much Gurbai or Makai can do but tell Kanalas that she must be firm with her mother.

The concerns are more dire at the next house. Erzsebet Orosz stands outside her two-room shack, one room of which is a corrugated tin enclosure draped with blankets. She is tending to a pile of tree branches for which she has just paid 50 euros for firewood and cooking. Gurbai and Makai want to check on Orosz, who is 38 and pregnant with her 10th child, and to see if she has gotten a birth certificate yet for her 1-year-old infant. She has.

But, she tells them, the baby she is carrying isn't moving. She had wanted an abortion, she mentions, but because she has had 25 already, the doctor refused to perform the procedure. As for birth control, she says she doesn't have the time or money to travel to the nearest town to get it—there is no family planning program in the community. And she can't leave her children on their own. "They almost burned the house down one day because they weren't careful," Orosz says.

(On a subsequent doctor's visit, with Makai and Gurbai in tow, Orosz learns that her unborn baby is fine.)

This part of the settlement is the picture of Europe's Third World poverty, full of makeshift housing, stray dogs, and underclothed babies. Nearly every woman of child-bearing age is pregnant, holding a small child, or both.

As they walk along, a man stumbles into his house. "I'm healthy, but I'm a little drunk," he yells out to Makai and Gurbai. Another man catches the eye of a visitor and points, half in exasperation and half in apology, to the muddy road that makes movement here so difficult.

Right Side of the Tracks

But when Gurbai and Makai reach the community school, things change. It is well-kept and warm. The walls are painted in cheerful pink and white, and covered with the students' artwork. Students in kindergarten and grades one through three attend this school with its new windows and desks. Gurbai and Makai stop by regularly to talk about hygiene and nutrition.

On this day, the third grade, which is learning English, serenades a visiting Anglophone with *My Bonny Lies Over the Ocean.*

It is as if the school separates the two parts of the community. Past the school, the houses are more substantial and cleaner. The road is still muddy, but less so, and a sidewalk is always available. An obvious class difference exists here.

Most striking is an immaculately kept, picket-fenced compound of two peach-colored houses, joined by a grapevine-covered courtyard. It could well be on a Mediterranean island. Gyorgy Varga, the owner, comes out to chat with Gurbai and Makai. Varga, 70, was a bricklayer in a nearby town for 35 years and retired with a pension. He grumbles that the poorer Roma here are simply unwilling to work.

In the midst of the conversation, a group of women carrying children approach. They are anxious about an outbreak of hepatitis in the community that they say started with the death of one man. Hepatitis and tuberculosis are common diseases here, Gurbai says. Residents here have received pills, but not shots to ward off hepatitis, Makai says.

"We told you and we told you to wash your hands," Gurbai tells them gently. "Tell your children they have to wash their hands."

A young woman, pregnant, protests. "I wash all the time! Look at me, I'm not dirty," she exclaims.

Another young woman says she went to the doctor for shots, who she says told her, "You don't need shots. You just need to wash yourselves."

"Gypsies are like other people," says one older woman, who suggests the source of the hepatitis outbreak is on the other side of the tracks. "We're clean but our children play with the other children. If my child gets hepatitis, I'll kill them."

Another woman joins the discussion from a distance, shouting, "They say we aren't civilized people, but look at these conditions! I paid for pipes to bring water to my house, but the mayor wouldn't approve it."

Now water is fetched from a common pump that constantly trickles into the road. Gurbai and Makai agree to tell the local council.

Makai explains later that water and sewer pipes have been approved for the community. A site for a water tower has already been excavated but work cannot move forward in the winter, she says.

So, maybe, by this time next year, things will be different. And there will likely be a few more children scampering through the mud.

Transitions Online, 27 January 2009

WE'RE NOT WORTHY

By Jeremy Druker

Why do Slovakia's politicians think its people need constant reminders that they should be proud of their country?

PRAGUE

By now, news of Slovakia's "patriotic act" has spread far and wide, even overshadowing a real event that instilled more patriotism among Slovaks than anything state-mandated could: the surprising success of the country's hockey team at the Olympics.

Critics at home and abroad have scoffed at the ambitions of the country's nationalists, led by the buffoonish Jan Slota of the Slovak Nationalist Party, to mandate that every school play the Slovak national anthem at the beginning of the week and that each classroom display a prescribed set of state symbols.

Much of the discussion has revolved around the foolishness of trying to "force" patriotism by legislative means; the natural antipathy of those raised under the communist regime toward any obligatory devotion to the state; and the cost of implementing the law when the Ministry of Education has already said it will not pay to outfit classrooms with the required symbols.

Yet less talk has been about the motivation of Slota and his fellow nationalists for even launching such a controversial initiative. Yes, Slota's party has dropped perilously in the polls after allegations of corruption and incompetence swirled around the party's ministers. The party elite apparently see the bill as a way to turn around the party's fortunes, especially as an opportunity to whip out its normal stable of anti-Hungarian rhetoric ("If [Slovakia's ethnic Hungarians] consider Hungary their homeland, that is the beginning of the end," Slota said).

But the other parties in the ruling coalition agreed to go along as well, including the powerful Smer party, led by Prime Minister Robert Fico. The legislation also, according to the *Slovak Spectator*, had the "silent consent of opposition MPs, most of whom despite their pronounced disagreement with the law did not raise their hands against it."

Clearly, a full 17 years after the peaceful breakup of Czechoslovakia, at least the politicians believe that a large part of the electorate still feels uncomfortable enough with Slovakia's independence (and correspondingly its short history) that they need the reinforcement of state symbols, anthems, and the like. Parents, they guessed, would want their children immersed in all of that paraphernalia so they would grow up to be loyal, proud Slovaks.

And they were counting on the majority of the population to simply accede to yet another "nation-building" move of the Fico government, which has worked arduously to link the Slovaks with a long-ago glorious past and strengthen the use of the Slovak language, including a controversial law passed in 2009 that included fines for not using the Slovak language in official communication.

To a large extent, such moves, including the patriotism bill, have one thing in common: a cynical supposition that Slovaks are so insecure, so beset by complexes about their little state and history of being ruled by foreign powers, that they will welcome the government's helping hand in making them proud of their country.

The outrage over the law—the petitions, the massive online protests, even a march through Bratislava by students and teachers, singing the national anthem—indicate the contrary. Tens of thousands of Slovaks have rebelled against the notion that they need the state to instill feelings of patriotism, especially as a weapon against supposed outside forces that threaten Slovakia's existence (i.e. a renewed Hungarian territorial threat, says Slota).

Feeling Groovy

In fact, according to Eurobarometer statistics released in January, most Slovaks are satisfied with their lives. While the EU average is 80 percent, Slovaks came in at 70 percent, only slightly behind Italy and far ahead of Greece, Hungary, and Bulgaria, which all ranked below 50 percent. Around 30 percent said things had gotten worse over the past five years, still below the EU average.

Those numbers aren't amazing, but they are solid for citizens of a young democracy and would seem to indicate that overall, Slovaks feel pretty good about their lives and their state. It would be hard to imagine people answering positively to the questions posed by the Eurobarometer team if they felt overly disappointed with their country or under threat from neighboring states or hordes of threatening minorities.

How then to reconcile those figures with numbers quoted in a recent article on Time.com that reported that "Slovaks do tend to have an astonishingly poor view of their nation"? The article referred to a 2006 study by the International Social Survey Program that placed Slovakia fourth from the bottom in a survey of patriotism in 33 countries.

One can only surmise that it might be years before most Slovaks start to view their personal success as a by-product, at least partially, of the state they live in and the country's remarkable transition in little more than a decade from being Central Europe's basket case (with former strongman Vladimir Meciar at the helm) to one of the region's success stories: entry into the EU and NATO, decent relations with its neighbors, and audacious economic and social reforms (until Fico started rolling back some of them).

Well aware of the backlash to the law, Fico has said that he advised President Ivan Gasparovic to veto it, so its passage can be delayed to allow schools more time to prepare for its implementation. The prime minister said he still agreed with the law's content, but chances are that the party felt it was wise to wait until after the June parliamentary elections before taking up the issue again.

That will be a bit soon for Slovaks' life satisfaction to translate into outright patriotism, but it should be enough time for Slota, so keen on promoting the national anthem, to actually learn its words. In an interview with journalists, he not only quoted the anthem inaccurately but also got the name of its author wrong.

Transitions Online, 19 March 2010

V. LANGUAGE LAB

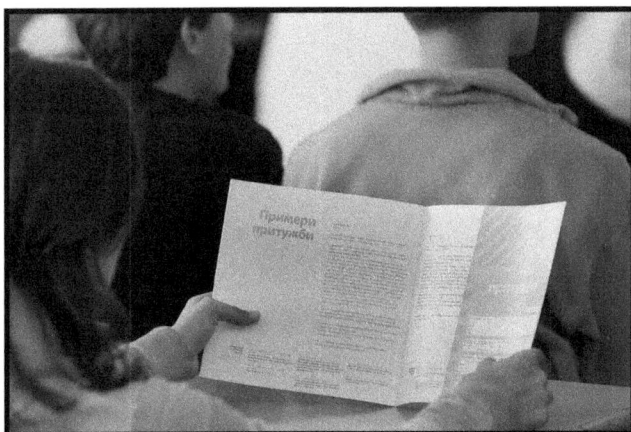

EXCHANGING WORDS

By *Ljubica Grozdanovska Dimishkovska*

Skopje's enthusiastic push for Macedonian language classes for Albanian first-graders leads to a schools boycott.

SKOPJE

Six-year-old Musa and his friend Vlatko live in the same apartment building and walk 40 meters to the same school every day. After school, they play together and have no trouble understanding each other. Their families celebrate holidays together.

But they don't go to school together. Musa is Albanian and his classes are taught in the Albanian language. Vlatko, a Macedonian, learns in his native language. Their school divides their classes into shifts.

At this point in their education, the first-graders are learning words and numbers through games and descriptions. They also take classes in English.

But they were caught in an awkward situation when the second school semester began in mid-January and the Education Ministry announced a change in the language curriculum for Albanian pupils. Instead of beginning their studies of the Macedonian language in the fourth grade, they must now start younger, in the first grade.

Many angry Albanian parents kept their children home from school. Musa's parents joined the boycott.

"We have nothing against the Macedonian language because we live in this country, and everyone in our family speaks the language," Sulejman Memeti, Musa's father, said. "We also have very good relationships with our neighbors. The only reason we decided to boycott the school system was because the majority of Albanian parents decided to."

Albanian Minority

According to state figures, about one-fourth of the population of Macedonia is Albanian. The internationally backed Ohrid Framework Agreement, which ended fighting between Albanian separatists and Macedonian security forces in 2001, grants Albanian–majority areas the right to education in their native tongue.

The ministry agreed to delay the change and students went back to school, but the government's plan has made a lot of people nervous, even in places where Albanians and Macedonians co-exist peacefully. Mustafa Fetahu, Musa and Vlatko's principal, began yelling when approached for a comment about it.

"I don't want to talk about this situation. The Education Ministry is responsible for this mess. They just want to experiment. If they would leave us alone, we know how to handle the situation," he said.

But it wasn't strictly the ministry's idea. The proposal was originally part of an effort to integrate education championed by the Organization for Security and Cooperation in Europe.

Education for Albanians and Macedonians has long run along parallel tracks, in different schools or in different shifts. Recently, many Albanian high-schoolers here have opted for universities in neighboring Kosovo or Albania.

But in January 2009, Knut Vollebaek, the OSCE's high commissioner on national minorities, gave a speech at the South East European University in Tetovo in which he called for a careful integration of Albanian and Macedonian education. While acknowledging the importance of including minority languages in the country's system of instruction, Vollebaek lamented that many young people were not learning Macedonian.

"As the result, many children don't speak the Macedonian language at all and this language can help them in their further professional and academic careers," Vollebaek said. "If this language segregation continues, in the long term, it might reflect on the stability of Macedonian society. Learning the Macedonian language as the official, state language doesn't mean that minority rights are less respected. Classes in the Macedonian language can be offered at the earliest age."

From that speech came a plan that envisioned education officials in Skopje working with experts from the OSCE to create a curriculum for Macedonian-language instruction for Albanian first-graders. The goal would be for the children to learn 200 expressions in that first year through game-playing.

Exchanging Blame

In a disputed account, Education Minister Nikola Todorov said the government decided to move forward with the plan in August, with an eye to implementing it in the beginning of the 2009-2010 school year or at the start of the second semester. But Abdulakim Ademi, the deputy prime minister whose portfolio includes implementation of the Ohrid accord, said the decision was made by Todorov himself. Ademi is a member of the Democratic Union for Integration, an Albanian party that is in a coalition government with the ruling VMRO-DPMNE party.

Because of the heightened tension on this issue, exactly one year after Vollebaek's speech in Tetovo, the high commissioner sent a letter to Prime Minister Nikola Gruevski suggesting that the project be delayed pending further study.

Vollebaek called for a dialogue between the concerned sides and emphasized the need for choosing appropriate teaching materials and for training teachers.

The next day, Todorov was defiant. "I don't plan to take some radical measures in order to implement the decision, but I won't back away from it," he said at a press conference. Referring to a court case seeking to have the proposal declared unconstitutional, he said, "I think we should judge if this decision is constitutional and legal through expert debate. I'll try to prove that this decision is scientifically and legally based."

That suit was filed by Realiteti, a Skopje-based watchdog group that looks out for the rights of Albanian students in Macedonia's education system. The group says most Albanians and Macedonians get along well but such political interference could change that. It supports the current parallel system of education.

Realiteti recently organized a second schools boycott to force administrators to keep student information in ethnically mixed schools in both languages. Currently it is recorded only in Macedonian.

Realiteti's director, Valjon Belja, said he was speaking on behalf of many Albanian parents. "We're reacting so strongly to this because Albanians in

Macedonia see this as having the majority language forced on them, and that creates resentment."

Belja acknowledged that many Albanian students don't speak Macedonian but said that's a problem of the education system overall.

"Albanian students from the fourth grade in primary till the fourth year in secondary education have enough time to learn the Macedonian language, but that's not the case because the students don't take it seriously. They see it as one of many subjects in their education and that's why they don't speak the language. The ministry must strengthen this segment," he said.

Members of the opposition Social Democratic Union said the government's move was clumsy and ill-thought out. "The government is probably doing this just to provoke tension at a very sensitive period for the country," said Andrej Petrov, vice president of the Social Democrats.

"If someone thinks that this will ease interethnic relations, then that's a lie. This is one more example of the government making policy on a daily basis without any long-term vision. It's a strong signal by VMRO-DPMNE to the Albanians that the only official language in Macedonia is Macedonian," Petrov said.

The country's constitution declares Macedonian, along with any other language spoken by at least 20 percent of the population, as the official language.

Mersel Bilali, a professor of international humanitarian law at the FON University in Skopje, said the real solution is a complete overhaul of the education system. He said the issue of interethnic tensions in Macedonia is a phony one, cooked up by politicians as a distraction from the country's real problems.

"I think there's no real resistance to learning the Macedonian language. It's more a reaction by the Albanian population to the nationalist policy of the ruling party. Unfortunately, Gruevski has a very low rating among Albanians," Bilali said.

Gruevski's VMRO-DPME has been on a campaign to boost national pride—some would say to fan the flames of nationalism—by claiming a glorious past for Macedonia that includes the planned erection of a statue of Alexander the Great in Skopje's central square and the naming of a stadium after Phillip II, Alexander's father. In addition, the party proposes to build an Orthodox church in the main square over the objections the country's Muslims, many of whom are Albanian, and it is an Orthodox priest, not an imam, who accompanies government officials to give his blessing when a new building is opened.

Bilali, who is Albanian, said the attempt at integrating education had been bungled. "With the proper analysis and approach, this project could succeed. In ethnically mixed environments it's not a sin, for instance, for Macedonians to start learning the Albanian language. In most institutions today people from different nationalities work together. If an Albanian comes to an office where Macedonians are working, and if they don't speak the language of the other, they have to find translators. Instead of wasting time and energy, they should have at least a basic knowledge of the languages."

Transitions Online, 15 March 2010

TONGUE-TIED SCHOOLS

By Hamid Toursunov

*Russian still dominates higher education but is slowly
disappearing from Kyrgyz schoolrooms.*

OSH, KYRGYZSTAN

The exodus of native Russian speakers out of Kyrgyzstan shows no
signs of slowing.

That is according to Eugene Breslavskiy, head of the Sodrujestvo
association of ethnic Russians. "Those who remain have doubts about their
future in this country," says Breslavskiy.

He says the association's mission "is to protect the Russian world—
that is, to preserve Russian culture, language and traditions." But in much
of Kyrgyzstan this is a rapidly disappearing world.

The Russian language, although still widely used by the Kyrgyz political
establishment and in higher education, is becoming an alien tongue to the
younger generation. Kyrgyzstan, where 20 years ago nearly one in every
three inhabitants spoke fluent Russian, is seeing the gradual extinction of
the language as its native speakers dwindle.

The outflow of Russian speakers, combined with earlier efforts in
support of the Kyrgyz language in education and government, have led to
a paradoxical situation. Because many young Kyrgyz now have little or no
exposure to Russian, they are virtually shut out of the universities owing to
the continued dominance of Russian in higher education.

Top Kyrgyz officials try to stem the outflow of Russian speakers, often
praising the Russian language and its important place in the multinational
country. In 2003, Kyrgyzstan became the only former Soviet Central Asian
republic to restore Russian as an official language.

The appointment of ethnic Russian Igor Chudinov as prime minister in 2007 was widely seen as another move to mollify Russian speakers.[9] But changes in Kyrgyzstan are reflected throughout the former Soviet Union, where laws were amended after independence to replace Russian as the mandatory language of government and education, and de-Russification policies triggered an exodus of ethnic Russians. English is increasingly competing with Russian as a preferred foreign language.

Around half of the officially denoted "ethnic Russians" have left Kyrgyzstan since independence and in southern Kyrgyzstan in particular, few young people know any Russian, although their parents and grandparents speak it well from their schooling in the Soviet period.

Since 1989, government jobs are reserved by law for those who can speak and write the Kyrgyz language.

"Russians are leaving the country because the law prohibits non-Kyrgyz speakers from working for the government," says Sadykjan Makhmudov, an Osh lawyer and human-rights activist.

"Although the Kyrgyz Constitution bans any infringement of human rights and freedoms based on lack of knowledge of the state [Kyrgyz] language, employment opportunities for non-Kyrgyz speakers are very few. What happens here in fact is that present law contradicts the constitution."

Russian's Last Bastion

The Education Ministry now acknowledges that this process is contributing to the deterioration of educational standards. Many young teachers are emerging from university with a less-than-perfect grasp of their major subjects owing to their faulty knowledge of Russian. In 2007, the ministry said that more than 60 percent of primary school children and at least 80 percent of secondary school students do not possess even basic knowledge of mathematics and demonstrate inadequate reading skills.

The universities remain a bastion of Russian partly because the Kyrgyz language is not yet equipped to handle abstract and technical concepts, a number of academics believe.

"The Kyrgyz language is not fulfilling its functions, that is, enlightenment and education. The language's capacity for scientific education is seriously limited," a professor from Kyrgyz-Turkish University in Bishkek—the name reflects the main languages spoken there—said in February, as quoted

113

by the 24.kg news site. Zamira Derbisheva also said that Russian continues to be used in scientific research, seminars, courses, theses and monographs.

Most Kyrgyz universities and vocational schools still use Russian as the language of instruction. Russian dominates in science and technology because Kyrgyz lacks many specialized terms, but is not confined to those fields. At Osh State University, authorities could not find a Kyrgyz equivalent for the Russian word meaning "art," so the Faculty of Arts bears the Russian title *iskusstvo*.

Another academic, Alexander Katsev of Kyrgyz-Slavic University, echoed such concerns at a roundtable in March on the role of the Russian language in Kyrgyzstan, stating that no important texts have been published in Kyrgyz since the country's independence.

The decline in use of Russian is putting many young people in double trouble. This is particularly true of those from rural and remote areas, who have limited or no access to higher education owing to their lack of Russian and who face a language barrier if they follow their many compatriots to Russia looking for work.

Today, according to official statistics, over 250,000 Kyrgyz labor migrants work in Russia. Unofficial estimates put the figure as high as 800,000 people, a staggering figure in a country with a population of 5 million. In the last few years, more than 100,000 Kyrgyz nationals have obtained Russian citizenship.

Russian Teacher Shortage

In August 2007, the then-minister of education, Kanybek Osmonaliev, admitted that a lack of books and teachers was keeping schools in remote areas from teaching Russian. In another sign that the decline of Russian is being noticed by official Bishkek, the Education Ministry in March 2008 announced the start of a program to build up the use of Russian in primary and secondary schools. The ministry said it was concerned that the language was losing its former high status.

Secondary teachers and observers point out that more and more parents want their children to get an education at Russian-language schools.

"Four Russian-language classes have started up at our school since 2004," says Sanobar Saidova, a teacher from an Uzbek-language primary school in Osh. "All Uzbek-language schools have similar classes," she says.

"More groups could have started, but it hasn't happened owing to the shortage of Russian language teachers," she added, illustrating a problem that is affecting schools countrywide.

The plunge in living standards following Kyrgyzstan's exit from the USSR stripped much of the prestige from the poorly paid teaching profession. Retiring teachers are often not replaced, particularly teachers of Russian as a second language. Many of those still on the job are elderly.

"I don't know what will happen tomorrow. More and more teachers either retire or leave our schools. Young teachers have poor [Russian] language skills and don't meet our requirements," said Svetlana Karpushkina, the principal of Osh's Russian language school No. 20.

"Our school badly needs teachers who know Russian well. Graduates of the Russian philology department of Osh State University cannot even speak Russian well," Karpushkina complains.

The dearth of teachers is aggravated by a shortage of textbooks. Many Kyrgyz schoolchildren are still learning from the same Soviet-era books their parents used.

Breslavskiy, head of the Sodrujestvo association of ethnic Russians, says the Education Ministry is not meeting schools' demand for new Russian texts. The ministry admits that a shortage of textbooks is a problem for schools teaching in all three of the country's main languages—Kyrgyz, Uzbek and Russian—and has earmarked new texts for the recently announced Russian-language teaching program.

The Multilingual South

Before the collapse of the Soviet Union, Kyrgyzstan was home to nearly a million ethnic Russians. The emigration of many of this community has made the 800,000 ethnic Uzbeks the second biggest ethnic group after the Kyrgyz.

Today observers assert that the Uzbek language is taking more an active position in Kyrgyzstan, particularly in the southern region.

Russian speakers are concentrated in Bishkek and the north. Estimates are that only 30,000 ethnic Russians still live in the three southernmost provinces bordering Uzbekistan. In contrast, the south is home to about 700,000 ethnic Uzbeks.

As use of Russian has dwindled, Uzbek has gained strength. Several television stations and newspapers use all three major languages, and for the past 10 years Uzbek speakers have been able to use their mother tongue at Kyrgyz–Uzbek University in Osh, Kyrgyzstan's second-largest city and the urban center of the southern provinces.

Historically, Uzbek-language schools have been common in Osh and Jalal-Abad provinces, so when Kyrgyz authorities wanted to bring in new teaching plans for Uzbek-language secondary schools that would have cut the amount of Uzbek used in classes, large protests by teachers forced Bishkek to cancel the policy.

Kyrgyz and Uzbek are related Turkic languages.

"When I speak Uzbek to Kyrgyz people, they speak Kyrgyz back to me. This way we easily communicate because it is easy for us to understand each other," says Azamjan Yakubov, a taxi driver from Jalal-Abad, a city near the Uzbek border.

Saidova, the Uzbek school teacher, says she also speaks the language at home and with friends and neighbors.

"Besides, we watch Uzbek language television every day, including the channels based in Uzbekistan," she says.

Long the prestige language in Kyrgyzstan, Russian still holds sway in the universities, the hospitals and many schools and even kindergartens despite official efforts to boost the standing of the Kyrgyz tongue. Both at home and in Russia where so many Kyrgyz citizens now work, knowledge of Russian is still seen as a prerequisite for success by many.

Saidova says she will send her three children to a Russian language school.

"A good knowledge of Russian will give my children more opportunities in the future," she says.

Transitions Online, 26 May 2008

TALKING
PAST ONE
ANOTHER

By Kseniya Pasechnik

Students in Crimea can learn in a variety of languages.
Most choose Russian.

SEVASTOPOL, UKRAINE

A range of possibilities are on offer to the students of Crimea, Ukraine's only autonomous republic. They can study in schools where all classes are taught in Ukrainian, or Russian, or Crimean Tatar. Or they can study in multilingual schools where different classes are taught in different languages.

Chances are, most will choose Russian-language schools, a reality that the government in Ukraine is trying to change, largely through financing Ukrainian-language education programs much more than those in Russian. That strategy has met with much local resistance.

The continuing dominance of Russian in Crimea, which is located on the northern coast of the Black Sea, is hardly surprising given that ethnic Russians make up 59 percent of the local population of just over 2 million, compared with 24 percent ethnic Ukrainians and 12 percent Crimean Tatars, according to the 2001 census.

Around half of the schools in Ukraine where classes are taught predominantly in Russian are located in Crimea, according the Ukrainian Education Ministry, and nearly all schools in Crimea—555 of 576—hold classes predominantly in Russian (the only exceptions being Ukrainian literature, language, and history classes).

"In Crimea only seven schools provide teaching [mainly] in Ukrainian," said Ivan Vakarchuk, the Ukrainian minister of education, at a recent press conference. "Only 7.3 percent of students receive their education in the country's official language, compared with 81.3 percent in the rest of the country. It is the lowest percentage in Ukraine."

According to the Education Ministry, not a single school in the rural areas of the Crimean peninsula provides instruction primarily in Ukrainian.

The minority Crimean Tatar population does not factor much in the linguistic debate.[10] A few schools in the Crimean district of Bakhchisaray, opened with funding from Ankara, conduct lessons only in Turkish, and some mosques offer Turkish-language instruction. But most Crimean Tatars study at ordinary institutions, in Crimean-Tartar language classes, if possible. If not, they receive their education in Russian or Ukrainian.

A Change in Tactics

Marina Chernysheva, a teacher at Yalta City School No. 4, contrasted the government's methods today with those of over a decade ago, under the presidency of Leonid Kuchma. In 1998, the authorities introduced measures to improve the study of Ukrainian in schools where other languages predominated by increasing the number of hours taught in Ukrainian. Looking back, Chernysheva views this policy as "soft" Ukrainization, encouraging the use of the language by linking it with a quality education.

"The best teachers, computers, textbooks, were sent to those classes. There were about eight students per class. Certainly, many children, even those who had previously been instructed in Russian, wanted to receive their education at those establishments," she said. "Since the quality of education in those classes was higher, Ukrainian was becoming more and more prestigious, as an increasing number of people wanted to study in Ukrainian-language schools. Separate lyceums and gymnasiums were created where teaching was conducted solely in Ukrainian."

Chernysheva and many others in Crimea feel the situation changed after the popular protests of the Orange Revolution at the end of 2004 helped usher in a more Western-oriented government. Now the talk is more of "forced Ukrainization."

"Linguistic pressure increased with the arrival of President Viktor Yushchenko," said Olga Orel, the mother of a Sevastopol schoolgirl.[11] "That has caused tension and resistance in pro-Russian Crimea." She said the local community, including the city council, opposed the Education Ministry's plans to open a Ukrainian-language gymnasium in Sevastopol.

Some students complain that they must study Ukrainian literature and Ukrainian history in Ukrainian only. "I want to learn about Russian history and literature. I don't need to study Ukrainian, and I'll receive a better university education [in the future] in Moscow," said Rustam Lebanov, an eighth-grader at a Simferopol city school.

Respondents to a poll conducted in June 2009 echoed those views. According to a survey of Crimean residents by the Kyiv-based Razumkov Center, 85.2 percent want their children to study in Russian-language schools. Only 4.4 percent desire a Ukrainian-language education and 2.8 percent an education in Crimean Tatar. An overwhelming majority—85.3 percent—believe that the Crimean population is exposed to forced Ukrainization.

Limited Authority

Others, however, call the supposed forced Ukrainization largely a myth cooked up by politicians. Georgiy Kasianov, director of education research at the International Renaissance Foundation in Kyiv, accuses the pro-Russian Party of the Regions as well as the Communist Party of playing the language card in their battles with political opponents, whom they mock as nationalists.

"When they speak about forced Ukrainization, they point to some decrees of the central government that were never implemented in Crimea, since the Kyiv-based Ministry of Education has no direct jurisdiction over Crimean education," Kasianov said. "As a rule, directives from Kyiv on 'Ukrainization' were never fulfilled," he added. As an autonomous republic, Crimea has its own parliament and ministries; only in extraordinary circumstances can the national government overrule their decisions.

Kasianov said the only way to change the situation is to make the Ukrainian language more attractive. "One example: the Ukrainian gymnasium that opened in Simferopol is extremely popular. It's funded directly from Kyiv and it has excellent premises and technical equipment. Every year there is a long line of parents, including Russians, who want to enroll their children there.

"There is no real state policy directed from Kyiv toward the Crimean educational sphere," he added. "It is mostly wishful thinking, decrees, and an endless stream of paper."

The More, The Better

In Crimea, locals counter Kyiv's arguments about the lack of Ukrainian instruction by insisting that educational programs adopted over a decade ago to foster cooperation among different ethnic groups are working. Under one such scheme, developed in 1996 by the Crimean Education Department, new schools with both Ukrainian and Crimean Tatar as languages of instruction were introduced. And, according to the department's annual analysis of the ethnic composition of students and interviews with parents, this program has helped to ameliorate the situation, in part by creating a situation where multi-language schools have become increasingly popular.

In the beginning, enrollment at such schools was considerably below average: only eight requests from parents in city schools and five from those in rural areas were enough to launch such classes. But as with the Ukrainian-language schools launched in the late 1990s, the low number of students per class was very attractive, allowing teachers to focus on particularly difficult concepts and spend more time on foreign languages. A report by the Crimean Department of Education and Science indicates substantial growth in the number of these classes over the last few years, from 264 in the 2002-2003 school year to 434 in 2004-2005, the last year for which data are available.

"Schools with multiple languages of instruction became a godsend in small settlements, where there is one school for everyone," said Alexander Gluzman, a former head of education in Crimea. As a result, children from all different nationalities have been able to study at such establishments.

TOL Chalkboard, 29 September 2009

VI. PROGRESS
REPORT

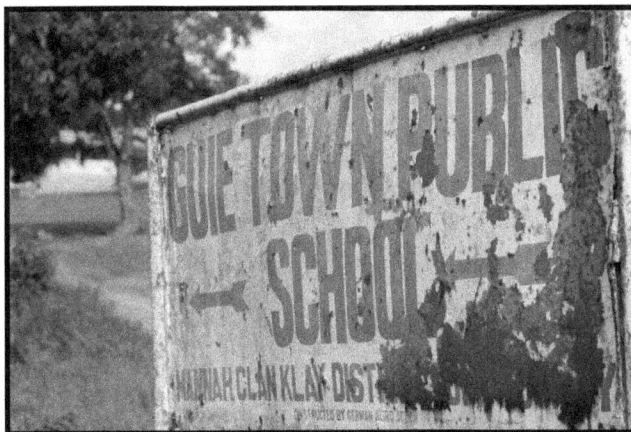

MACABRE MARKET

By Ljubica Grozdanovska Dimishkovska

Skopje's medical students are buying bones stolen from graves.
They say they have no other choice.

SKOPJE

Like a character in a crime movie, Olga walked through the dark alleys of the city's Taftalidje district late one February night. Waiting in the shadows was a person whose name she didn't know. Olga had made a deal with him on the phone a few days before to buy a human skull.

"I don't know this person. I don't know what he looks like or how he will provide the skull," said Olga, whose name was changed to protect her identity. "It was his idea to meet here in these alleys, and he insisted that it must be in the evening. I'm so afraid."

Trade in human bones is illegal in Macedonia, so medical students like Olga turn to the black market to acquire skulls and other bones for hands-on home study of human anatomy. Students at the Medical Faculty of Sts. Cyril and Methodius University in Skopje aren't allowed to take the medical school's bones home.

The risk of being caught buying bones is negligible, students say, compared with the possibility of failing the difficult anatomy exam that is required to receive a medical degree.

Students find bone dealers through friends at school. Most of the bones come from undertakers who steal them to sell.

"Almost all students at the faculty buy bones from undertakers," Olga said. "There are rumors that some undertakers dig into old and abandoned graves—graves that no one visits anymore. A whole network has developed. Students from Skopje buy bones from graveyards in Bitola and vice versa, so no one can track them."

When the day came for Olga to buy the skull, she almost didn't go through with it. One thought encouraged her not to back out.

"I have to buy a real human skull because that is the only way I can study and pass this exam," Olga said.

After 20 minutes of suspenseful waiting, the bone dealer finally showed up. He told Olga the skull would cost 50 euros.

"The most important thing is that you shouldn't say where you got it because we both will be in trouble," the man said. He told Olga that if she needed more bones, she should let him know a few weeks in advance. A bone would cost between 15 and 20 euros.

"Think about it," the man said.

Olga pulled 50 euros from her pocket, and the man handed over a black plastic bag he took from his car before driving away.

Nervously, Olga clutched the plastic bag, but she didn't dare open it until she was far away from the scene.

She opened the bag as soon as she got home. The skull was only chipped in a few places. Olga judged that it must have belonged to a young woman.

The Real Thing

Medical students in Macedonia insist that they need to have real skulls and other bones at home for study because the practice they get with them in the classroom is insufficient.

Professors recommend that they buy plastic replicas. But students say the alternatives aren't good enough—even though they cost less than the real thing. A plastic skull costs around 30 euros.

"The plastic skulls don't have all the details that we need to know if we want to pass the anatomy exam. So we are forced to buy real ones," Olga said.

After examining her acquisition, Olga said the skull she had purchased was not in as good a condition as it should have been. Nevertheless, she was happy she finally had one.

Most skulls sold on the black market are dug straight from the grave and are often dirty or broken, which makes them difficult to study.

Many students have to prepare their purchased skulls for study by themselves. Students often re-sell their bones after taking the exam.

A 32-year-old graduate from the Skopje Medical Faculty who spoke anonymously said he once bought a poorly preserved skull from an undertaker near the town of Bitola. It cost him 30 euros.

"I paid a cheap price, but I had to do a lot of work on it," he said.

He boiled the skull in salt water and filled it with corn. He said this ensures that the bones of the skull and their edges are distinct.

"I finished by painting it with a transparent layer" to give the skull its sheen, he said.

A Public Secret

Representatives of several cemetery management companies did not want to comment on the reports of a black market in bones. Some, however, said they had no evidence of cemetery workers re-opening graves.

A number of undertakers and cemetery workers in Skopje, Bitola, and other towns approached for this article declined to talk about the bone trade. A staff member of the Skopje medical school said school authorities are aware of the situation, but didn't know how to handle it. The staff member declined to give any other information regarding the illegal trade in bones.

A few months ago, Skopje police found a bag full of bones near the Lepenec River. Forensics showed the bones were several decades old. Authorities never found the owner of the bag, nor could they determine why the bones were there.

According to the Ministry of Internal Affairs, there are no official cases of bone stealing. Ivo Kotevski, a ministry spokesman, said authorities aren't sure how to handle what he called the "public secret" of the illegal bone market, because while everyone knows it exists, there is no tangible proof of it.

So public is the secret that it is even mentioned in a film called *Shadows*, directed by Milcho Manchevski. In the movie, released in 2007, a young male doctor is haunted by ghosts. The bones of the four ghosts (a beautiful girl, a middle-aged man, a baby, and an old lady) had been collected from a cemetery in a deserted village. The man's mother, who is also a doctor, had purchased the bones of the "shadows" illegally from an undertaker.

Olga keeps the skull she bought on her desk. It is the first thing that she sees every morning when she wakes up.

She has taped red and blue wires to it to represent blood vessels and nerves. "You can't learn this on a plastic skull. That is why I needed the skull so much," Olga said.

She hasn't yet decided what to do with the skull when she's done with it. And while she isn't worried that she'll be haunted by a ghost, Olga is curious to know whose skull she bought.

"It's creepy but dazzling, and you never seem to stop asking yourself to whom it belonged," she said. "How did this person die? Did she die from natural causes or violently? How old was she when she died?"

Transitions Online, 17 March 2008

VILLAGE KINDER-GARTENS STRUGGLE TO SURVIVE

By Claudia Ciobanu

Romania's rural schools are suffering from underfunding, neglect, and the government's budget priorities.

HARMAN, ROMANIA

A recent renovation brought new furniture and clean, bright bathrooms to Harman village's Kindergarten No. 1. But the daily maintenance of this four-room school for 87 children in Brasov County is complicated by financial difficulties that are not apparent to the casual visitor, but are all too common to many rural schools in Romania.

"We're not independent financially," said Oana Urdea, a teacher at the school.

At the end of 2005, the Romanian government began to transfer the burden of education funding from the central to local governments. The change was supposed to make the chronically underfinanced school system more efficient.

Over the past five years, successive governments have committed to giving 6 percent of GDP to education but have rarely managed to allocate more than two-thirds of that.

The money is not enough and even its allocation is not as flexible as the decentralization legislation makes it sound. The village primary school allocates local funds to the two kindergartens in Harman.

"We draw up a list of needs at the beginning of each academic year and the school grants us a sum of money for those expenses," Urdea said.

"If an unexpected expense appears during the year—a door or a window gets broken, for example—we need to make another request to the school and we will get the money ... sooner or later," the teacher explained. "The problem is that we can't really manage our own needs because we don't have direct access to any funds."

"We're in desperate need of a copy machine, for example, but we won't get it any time soon," she said.

Children and parents pose for a group photo at Brasov's Kindergarten No. 17. Children in city schools like this one typically enjoy much better facilities than their rural peers.

Private Help for Public Schools

Harman is a relatively well-off village of 4,500 people in Transylvania, the most prosperous part of Romania. But even if the village is not poor, Urdea says it is impossible to get additional funding from parents, a common practice in city schools.

"Some parents even find it hard to keep up with buying notebooks and pencils, the basic necessities," Urdea said. "I found the same situation in Harman as in another village where I worked, Racos. The parents are often unemployed, so it's out of the question to ask them for help with buying the necessary materials."

The decentralization promoted by the government—in line with European Union trends in education—has led to more funds being channeled by municipalities toward larger schools and those that have the ability to attract additional private financial support. Most of those schools are in urban centers.

Although decentralization was intended to make school financing more efficient, the change "is likely to put significant pressure on small village schools, which lack the number of students needed to secure adequate funds under the new system," according to a 2009 study by an independent body, the EU Monitoring and Advocacy Program. EUMAP monitors the performance of EU states and potential new members in the fields of human rights and the rule of law.

One beneficiary of this reform is Kindergarten No. 66 in Brasov. Located at the foot of the mountains that surround the historic city, the modern school for 270 children has 15 large well-equipped classrooms and special activity rooms. This year, the school received money for a new heating system from the local budget.

The excellent facilities at this publicly funded neighborhood kindergarten could be taken as an example of the success of Romanian authorities in providing quality education.

In reality, parents' contributions are vital.

"Romanian legislation requires us to register primarily children from the neighborhood and we do register them, but usually we make sure to also register children from other neighborhoods if we know that the parents are well-off and they could provide funds for the kindergarten," said Maricica Ganea, a teacher at the kindergarten.

"I rely heavily on funds provided by the parents and on their cooperation. We've been buying beds, curtains, and teaching materials with money given as voluntary donations by parents," Ganea said.

"When our city receives visits from EU officials, they're brought here to see the successes of Romanian education," the teacher continued. "And this is indeed a success. But it's not representative of the education system in our country."

Ganea explained that much relies on the teachers' own ability to gather funds.

"Last year, our kindergarten won 10,000 euros from a foodstuffs producer because I entered my class in an artistic competition and they won," she said. "It meant many hours of work on my part with the parents' help."

Teachers in the countryside are less likely to put in this commitment, the teacher continued.

"From my own experience in working at rural schools, I know that many of us were there on our way to better positions in the cities. We were in the villages for a year or two. We were unhappy with the working conditions, but few of us did anything to improve our material base or to include the parents more in the process of education."

Vanishing Village Kindergarteners

Teachers in village schools are usually very young, in their first years of professional life, or even unqualified. Teaching positions are distributed on the basis of an annual nationwide examination: teachers with higher scores and more experience go to city schools while those less prepared and younger end up in villages, until they improve their scores in subsequent exams.

According to Mihaela Manole, project coordinator with the Romanian branch of the charity Save the Children, poor teacher motivation is one of the most serious problems in Romanian schools, along with "insufficient investment in education and the excessive politicization of the educational field that translates into incoherent policies that shift with every new government coming to power."

All these problems are amplified in rural areas.

According to Save the Children, the number of working kindergartens in Romania plummeted from 7,616 in 2003 to 1,731 in 2007. Most of the kindergartens that closed were in rural areas.

In 2007, when a then-record amount of money was allocated from the national budget to education (1.5 billion lei, or 350 million euros, in infrastructure funding for pre-university education), the government blamed local authorities for poor management of funds and inadequate repair works that prevented many rural schools from opening for the new academic year.

"It is unacceptable that six months after the money was allocated from the national budget, not a penny of it was used by some localities," said then-Minister of Education Cristian Adomnitei.

Rural kindergartens and schools are closing not because of a specific policy decision but rather as one consequence of a series of measures meant to make education financing more efficient.

On top of the decentralization of school financing, in early 2009, the Education Ministry ordered the number of teachers countrywide to be cut. Hundreds of unqualified teachers, especially from rural areas, have been dismissed since, in many instances leading to schools closing down.

Education Minister Ecaterina Andronescu insisted that solutions could be found to keep children in class even with many schools closing. "We cannot simply close the schools and not care what happens to the pupils," the minister declared in August 2009. "We must see whether there is transportation so they can travel to the larger villages where they can have access to one teacher per classroom."

Reform Favors Cities

In reality, the closing of rural kindergartens and schools has taken its toll on the educational process. Children of different ages are often forced to follow the same course. In Kindergarten No. 1 in Harman (a village that is home to Romanian and German speakers), 20 German-speaking children of all ages are grouped together because the institution cannot afford the staff for three different age groups. Romanian children usually attend kindergarten (*gradinita*) for three or four years before starting the first grade.

The problem is likely to become more severe, with more than 15,000 teaching jobs on the chopping block. Those affected will be young teachers or pensioners doing extra hours, many of whom work in rural schools.

The other serious consequence is that pupils and teachers in some areas have to travel long distances to get to school, even on foot over mountain paths.

Manole, of Save the Children, said that in addition to such challenges, "Rural schools often lack basic facilities, such as heating during the winter, running water, or working toilets.

"Even more, poverty in rural areas forces families to use children to work in the fields, which takes priority over education."

The result of all the strains placed on rural kindergartens and schools has been an increase in dropout rates in rural areas. According to the Education Ministry, dropout rates have tripled since the late 1990s among some vulnerable social categories, such as children from rural areas, from poor families in the cities, and Romani children.

The primary-school dropout rate for rural areas tripled from 0.6 percent in the 2000-2001 academic year to 1.8 percent in 2006-2007. More than the percentages, the trend is worrisome to educators.

The new government says it intends to build 700 new kindergartens as an answer to the overcrowding of city schools that has grown worse as birth rates have risen in recent years. But some are skeptical of yet another government promise to spend more money on schools.

"It's unlikely that they will achieve this much," said Ganea, the kindergarten teacher from Brasov, echoing comments by commentators and opposition politicians. "And even if they do build new kindergartens, they'll do it in places like the center of Bucharest or the center of Brasov, where demand for places exceeds supply. This will not do much for rural areas."

Transitions Online, 13 January 2010

NEW MODEL, OLD PROBLEMS

By Farruh Yusupov

With the help of substantial foreign aid, Uzbekistan has poured cash into its educational sector in recent years, but challenges persist.

TASHKENT

With one-third of its population under the age of 15, Uzbekistan has had little choice but to spend millions of dollars on education reforms since the mid-1990s.

Despite an increase in funding and structural changes, the system remains mired by problems inherited from the Soviet period and the early years of independence, including low teacher salaries, petty corruption, and frequent interruptions to children's studies.

Two complementary programs form the basis of Uzbekistan's reformed national education model. In 1996, the government introduced the National Program on Personnel Training, which aimed to extend compulsory education from nine to 12 years—nine years of basic education followed by three years of secondary training in specialized lyceums and colleges. In 2004, Uzbekistan launched the first phase of the National Program for School Education Development, shifting the focus of reforms to improving the overall quality of education through new schools, renovations, and equipment.

Sharifboy Ergashev, head of the educational development department at the Education Ministry, says that both programs have so far proven successful.

"Hundreds of academic lyceums and vocational colleges have been built in every region of the country. They have been equipped with skilled personnel and meet the new requirements," Ergashev said. He also said that Uzbekistan is a pioneer in Central Asia in the implementation of these reforms.

Dilnara Isamitdinova, the World Bank country officer for Uzbekistan, agrees that, on the whole, the government's implementation of the National Program for School Education Development has been successful and the program is beginning to show positive results after a few initial hitches.

"The first phase of the program implemented by the ministry was a little slow in the beginning, because they needed to hire consultants and accomplish other tasks, but now it is in full swing," Isamitdinova said. "There have been some delays in procuring materials for the schools, but that's because the whole timetable was shifted by a bit."

Ergashev would not say how much money has been spent so far on implementing the national programs. But the UN's Human Development Report for Uzbekistan estimates that public expenditures on education exceeded 10 percent of the country's GDP, based on government data. The GDP in 2009 was $33 billion.

Foreign organizations have contributed to the effort. In 2007, the World Bank provided $15 million in loans for a project focusing on training teachers, improving educational resources, fostering community participation in education, and creating more efficient education budgets. The bank plans on lending another $25 million for the second phase of the project.

The U.S. Agency for International Development provided technical assistance to the tune of more than $1 million between 2004 and 2007. Besides these donors, the Asian Development Bank and Islamic Bank, as well as the South Korean and Chinese governments, have provided funds for programs to improve school libraries and train teachers in interactive teaching techniques.

However, after the events in Andijan in May 2005, when Uzbek forces opened fire on peaceful demonstrators, killing scores of people, the government kicked foreign organizations out of the country in response to a wave of international criticism. Some education projects funded by international donors ground to a halt. For example, USAID's Participation, Education, and Knowledge Strengthening basic education program, which focused on the development of a training course for primary and secondary teachers, was discontinued in 2006 on direct orders from the Uzbek government.

Under the new system, each student is supposed to choose which lyceum or vocational school he or she wishes to attend upon graduating from basic school. "Starting from kindergarten, the skills and talents of every single student will be monitored until the ninth grade, when they will receive a psychological-pedagogical summary and a recommendation for which school they should attend," Ergashev said. Students then select a school based upon their own interests and abilities.

But not everyone is so enthusiastic. "So far we have only seen the side effects of the reforms," said Rohilya, a teacher in the Syrdarya region who spoke on the condition that her real name not be used. "Basically, we now have a nine-year system because most children are deprived of the opportunity to continue their studies in the field of their choice." She was referring to complaints that not all students manage to get into the best lyceums or pursue their desired type of secondary education under the new system.

"Of course, after the ninth grade, the teachers are required [by district education authorities] to enroll children in any lyceum or college," Rohilya said. In most cases, students simply go to the schools that have free places, not the schools they want to attend. "Many children attend the last three years of the 12-year education system just because they are required to," she said.

Opportunities for Graft

The new education model created more opportunities for corruption, said Rohilya, because only the children of families who can afford to bribe teachers and administrators at the more prestigious lyceums and colleges are able to secure places in these schools and thus improve their chances of being admitted to university. Since many Uzbek families want their children to study law, medicine, or any field that would ensure a white-collar job, places in secondary schools that prepare students for these professions are highly coveted.

Unlike universities, which admit students based upon the results of strictly controlled standardized tests administered by the state, academic lyceums and colleges hold their own entrance examinations, creating

134

opportunities to manipulate the results. Regardless, the competition to get into these schools is fierce.

"Last year, many children from my school wanted to go to a medical college in the Hovost district," Rohilya said. "But most of them failed, and because they are required to continue to study, they ended up in colleges that nobody wants to go to, like construction colleges, which train them to be builders or plumbers. I would not want my own child to go there," she said.

Ergashev of the Education Ministry admits that not every one of the more than 600,000 students finishing secondary classes can choose a school according to field of interest. "But at least they have a profession in case they are not able to enter university," he said.

The new model has also done little to settle old disputes between Uzbekistan and the country's ethnic Tajiks, who form 5 percent of the country's population of 27 million. Tajiks are considered the country's second largest official minority, after Russians, yet neither of the two national education reform programs includes any activities directly targeting this community. Only 1.7 percent of Tajik schoolchildren studied in Tajik-language schools last year, according to the Education Ministry. The number of Tajik schools has steadily declined since the mid-1990s, with more than 50 Tajik schools closed down just in the last four years due to Uzbekistan's bad relations with neighboring Tajikistan.

Another side effect of the new system is that schoolchildren now have to rent their textbooks. Under the old system, schools were supposed to provide textbooks for free.

"For most families who are struggling to make ends meet, this extra expense is too much," said Zamira, a teacher whose name has also been changed to protect her identity out of concern for reprisals from the authorities. She is from the Oltiarik district of the Ferghana region.

Zamira's husband is also a teacher, and it is their duty to collect the money for textbook rentals. "We distribute the books to children and it becomes a big problem when we have to collect the rent. Many families cannot afford to pay, and I understand them. I have four children and for each of them we have to spend an extra 7,000–8,000 soms [less than 4 euros] for book rentals. With our family's modest income, it is an extra burden for us," she said.

However, both Rohilya and Zamira say that the income from the book rental system allows schools to provide all the necessary textbooks to their students.

The increase in funding for education in recent years has not translated into higher wages for Uzbek teachers. An average teacher earns the equivalent of 50 euros per month, though President Islam Karimov has claimed the average pay is far higher.

"My monthly salary and that of my husband are merely enough for a bag of flour and other basic foods," Zamira said. "The low income of teachers makes the profession quite unpopular among young people and does not inspire teachers to develop their skills."

In the last 10 years or so, a large number of educators have switched to other professions. Many are now engaged in unskilled labor, working in markets or driving taxis. Some have long since left for Russia or Kazakhstan as labor migrants.

Such modest salaries also contribute to the persistence of corruption in Uzbekistan's public schools.

Rohilya, the teacher, believes that reforms will yield results sooner if those who are directly affected by the changes had a voice. "Because the national programs lack one important thing—feedback from teachers and students, who are the main players in this new system—it feels like we, teachers and pupils, are the subjects of an experiment, and it is very difficult to predict when it will be a success."

TOL Chalkboard, 9 June 2009

NO ROOM
FOR SEX
EDUCATION

By Tamar Kikacheishvili

The subject remains outside the curriculum in Georgian schools.

TBILISI

Andro Chitadze is a 16-year-old high school student at public school No. 61 in Tbilisi. Like his classmates, Chitadze gets his information about sex everywhere except in the classroom.

"Usually, information about sex is available on the street, from friends and older guys who are experienced in this. Some of my friends buy newspapers and magazines to read about sex, others use the Internet [for information]," said Chitadze.

His mother believes that sex education plays an important role in the psychological development of a child, and this should not be ignored by the schools. "Sometimes Andro has many questions about this issue and I'd feel better if the psychologist would explain it to him in more professional and understandable language. I'm all for sex education at schools, but the methods should be well-thought-out," Irma Chitadze said.

But sex education remains a taboo subject in this socially conservative nation. According to Simon Janashia, who heads the National Curriculum and Assessment Center at the Georgian Ministry of Education and Science, there is no appropriate subject on the curriculum that could integrate sex education. "There is some information about this in the biology course, but there is very little," Janashia said.

The main reason why sex education has not been incorporated into the curriculum is widespread opposition from religious leaders and the public.

"Most of the parents at our school are against sex education for different reasons, but the major reason is religion. Our religion, Orthodox Christianity, forbids this kind of knowledge being given to students," Irma Chitadze said.

Child psychotherapist Zaza Vardiashvili argues that sex education not only contributes to a lower number of abortions, but also decreases the transmission of sexually transmitted diseases among teenagers. (The number of abortions among 15- to 19-year-olds rose from 1,037 in 2007 to 1,359 in 2008, according to the national statistics office.)

The best option for conveying lessons about reproduction, says Vardiashvili, is for parents to discuss sexual issues with their children. However, she doesn't feel that Georgian parents are ready for this.

"They simply don't know how, or they feel too ashamed to speak about this issue with their children. I think it would be good if psychologists trained the parents," said Vardiashvili.

Vardiashvili points out that there are different opinions within the psychology profession in Georgia regarding the sex education. Some psychologists advocate that sex education should be integrated into related subjects on the curriculum, while others believe that sex education should be a separate course.

"I think that a school psychologist should lead this course for children in the age groups 10, 11, 12 and 13. At the beginning of the course, they should cover the anatomical differences between females and males as a preparation to discussing physical changes. Then, for students aged 11 to 12, they should teach about intimate relations between females and males and, at the age of 12-13, sexual hygiene," Vardiashvili said.

The only Georgian book on sex education, *Joyful Speeches about Sex*, was published more than a decade ago. The publisher, Anna Chabashvili, director of the Diogene publishing house, remembers the wave of protests when the book was released. "People were calling and some came to our office demanding that we take the book off the shelves. It was a real scandal," Chabashvili said.

One of the authors, Tamar Lebanidze, is a professional psychologist. She claims that the book's negative reception was due to the fact that "people see danger where there is no real danger. This problem was caused by the lack of information [about sex] at the time. Most of [those expressing negative opinions] did not even read this book. However, we also received some positive calls. People were in a hurry to express their opinions, both negative and positive."

Lebanidze said the most forceful opinions came from Orthodox Christian parents. Some 83 percent Georgians identify themselves as Orthodox Christian.

Religious Objections

Episcopes Ioane, who heads the Patriarchy of Georgia's education center, says the position of the Orthodox Church on sex education is not so rigid, but he does believe that the family should be responsible for educating children about sexual issues.

"This information should be given to children on an individual basis," he said. "I think that there should be centers for the parents where they will be taught how to explain sex to their child, considering his or her individual characteristics."

Views about sex education in public schools are mixed among minority faiths.

Tsitsino Khitarishvili works at the Sulkhan-Saba Orbeliani Institute of Theology, Philosophy, Culture and History in Tbilisi. A Catholic, Khitarishvili believes that sex education is an important element in family planning. "We are against abortion, and sex education will provide students with information that may decrease the number of abortions. People need knowledge [about sex] before they begin having it," Khitarishvili said.

The Georgian Catholic Society has a center for sex education in Kutaisi but this is only for adults. "The trainings there inform young people about sex. I think it would be good if there were the same centers for teenagers," Khitarishvili said.

Iasin Aliev is an imam at Tbilisi's Juma mosque. He believes the authorities do not have the right to put sex education on the curriculum in schools where Muslim students study. "The Koran includes all important information about human relations," Aliev said.

Shalva Tetruashvili, chairman of the Jewish Sephardic Organization in Tbilisi, argues that the family should educate the child, but adds that "two, three months before marriage, young people can go to the rabbi and he will explain to them about the issues of relationship between man and woman."

TOL Chalkboard, 9 November 2009

SCHOOLS ON EDGE

By Igor Jovanovic

Serbia's new education law sparks fears of massive teacher layoffs.

BELGRADE

New exit exams for elementary school students, the introduction of Romani teaching assistants, an equal starting point for all children—all were big changes brought about by Serbia's new education law. But all remained in the shadow of heated debates about financing, looming school closures, and possible layoffs.

All the leading teachers' unions had announced a strike over the new law, passed by parliament only at the end of August 2009, which stipulates that schools will no longer be financed according to the number of students, but according to the number of classes they offer.

This was a budget-cutting measure the World Bank had proposed in a study it conducted on the Serbian school system. Local media reported that the World Bank recommended that Serbia should have 30 students per class on average, merging smaller classes and terminating 11,000 classes overall in an effort that would save approximately 150 million euros per year. That would all be a prelude, the unions argued, to teacher dismissals.

Such austerity measures come amid a deepening economic crisis that has forced Serbia to seek out a loan of 2.9 billion euros from the International Monetary Fund. As a condition for closing a credit arrangement, the IMF demanded that the authorities make drastic cuts in public spending and increase taxes, as well as implement the World Bank recommendation on school financing.

Believing that a tax hike would ruin the national economy, the government instead proposed state administration cuts, including the dismissal of employees in government, health care, and education. Prime

Minister Mirko Cvetkovic said Serbia has some 14,000 excess employees in the three sectors.

That made teachers fear even more for their jobs. In the end, Education Minister Zarko Obradovic managed to convince the unions that the new method of financing would not be implemented before 2013, by which time several pilot projects would have been carried out to monitor the potential impact of the new system. Obradovic said the cuts demanded by international lenders did not necessarily envisage the dismissal of employees, but rather proposed that money could also be saved through the redistribution of funds within the existing budget. He told reporters he disagreed with the World Bank recommendation that Serbian classes should have 30 students each, since the average number per class in EU countries was between 18 and 26.

Bigger Classes

However, at the beginning of the new school year, schools received instructions saying that first- and fifth-grade classes in elementary schools could only be divided up into smaller classes if they had 34 students or more. While not officially part of the new school financing plan, the move appears to be the first major step in that direction. The authorities apparently chose these grades, because they represent the least level of disruption. Children start school in the first grade, and after four years with a single teacher, they start attending classes in the fifth grade taught by a number of different teachers.

The decision has caused dissatisfaction among parents, who believe that their children will not get a proper education in big classes.

"We know the state has to save money, but do children have to suffer because of it?" asked Bosko Matic, the father of a first-grade student in Belgrade. "Besides, what kind of savings will there be in the end, if they are made in the education of future generations? How can a teacher devote sufficient attention to students when there are more than 30 in a class? The teacher will not have enough time to even check their knowledge regularly, let alone develop their talents."

Leonardo Erdelji, head of the Association of Teachers Unions of Serbia, said he agreed with Obradovic that funds could be found elsewhere and not necessarily result in teacher dismissals. In an interview, he said that the union knew that a number of employees who were supposed to retire were still working. Just their retirement would lead to big savings, he said.

"We have also asked the government not to employ new people in schools," Erdelji said. "If a new employee is needed, they should first be sought among the employees in a school who are or may become redundant …. Also, redundant teachers can switch to the adult education system."

Demographically Challenged

But demographics are not in favor of the teachers. According to Erdelji's association, more than 812,000 students attended elementary schools in Serbia in 1990-1991 with the average number of students per class at 25.35. By 2006-2007, however, only 622,562 students were attending elementary schools and the average had sunk to 20.70 students per class. Part of the decline can be attributed to emigration and conflicts that ensued the collapse of the old Yugoslavia, but Serbia's birth rate is also declining.

An elementary teacher from Belgrade, speaking on condition of anonymity, said that her school had terminated one class due to too few students, resulting in the decision to lay off one teacher.

"It was very stressful," she said. "Prior to the dismissal, they gave points to each first- to fourth-grade teacher in the school. Points were given for everything—whether we have children, whether our spouse is employed, whether we have written a textbook, how many years we have been working…. In the end, a female colleague of mine with the smallest number of points was dismissed."

And in Serbia's current economic malaise, with current unemployment at around 13.5 percent, finding a new job is no easy task.

But Vigor Majic, director of Petnica, an education center for gifted high school students, thinks that the Education Ministry could have cited certain articles of previous laws earlier in order to create larger classes or shut down small schools instead of relying on outside pressure to do so.

"Whether there will be dismissals and to what extent is not a matter of the law, but of political will and intentions," Majic said. "I think that the education system in Serbia contains an excessive number of unsuccessful and bad teachers—be they unmotivated or undereducated, or whatever the reason may be. But even if the system manages to recognize and dismiss them, the question is—who will replace them?"

Majic added that the Serbian education system does a poor job at motivating the country's best students to excel either at the elementary or high school level.

Other provisions of the new education law received far less press than the debates over class size and possible layoffs, but also represented major changes, including an entirely new process for entering high school. Students who started the seventh grade this fall will take a mandatory final exam once they finish their elementary education (after the eighth grade), instead of just an enrollment test for high school. Based on that exam, children will qualify for high schools according to their points.

"We will see how the schools prepare their students for that exam— the results of teachers and schools will also be monitored rather than just the children's work," Education Ministry State Secretary Tinde Kovac-Cerovic said. The aim of the new test, she said, is to not only monitor the understanding of learned knowledge, but also its application. Initially students will have to take tests only in Serbian and mathematics, and the list of subjects will gradually increase.

Another important novelty is that the new law is meant to facilitate all children attending mainstream schools. "Children will no longer be prevented from starting school because they do not speak the language, have no personal ID, or because they do not demonstrate sufficient knowledge in pre-enrollment tests," Kovac-Cerovic said.

In the past, children that didn't pass pre-enrollment tests were mostly sent off to special schools, leading to many Roma children being forced to attend educational institutions targeted for mentally disabled children. Now Romani children will have teaching assistants to further their development.

Education Minister Obradovic told the Belgrade media that the new law and the Romani assistants would help increase the number of Romani children in the education system, adding that help was also required of the Romani community and associations.

"The fact is that the number of Roma in preschools and at all other education levels is far below what is necessary," Obradovic said. "Over 60 percent of the Roma in Serbia have an elementary school diploma. Some 7.8 percent have finished high school, whereas only 0.3 percent have graduated from college or university."

Despite all the positive changes touted by the Education Ministry, Majic from Petnica center thinks the new law is no guarantee for widespread improvement.

"The quality of education is ensured by a mix of good programs, good teachers, and a good system. That cannot be seen clearly in this law, which mostly focuses on strong state control of the work of schools and teachers and very little on stimulating quality initiatives, innovation, and good results," he said.

Majic believes that Serbia will be nowhere near the education standards of developed countries for many years with just this law. "Education is not a societal development priority here. The majority of faculties also offer a poor and dysfunctional education—hence the appearance of better teachers cannot be expected any time soon," he said.

TOL Chalkboard, 22 December 2009

EDUCATION ON STRIKE, EDUCATION AT STAKE

By Tanya Obushtarova

Massive teachers' strikes forced the Bulgarian government to hasten reforms, but stopped short of fixing the school system.

SOFIA

Many high school students were in the front lines of the January 2009 protests in Sofia, when a peaceful rally against government corruption and the slow pace of reforms erupted into a violent clash between marchers and police.

Several 16-year-olds were arrested. Though many were impressed with the civic consciousness of high school students taking to the streets, others found themselves asking: Why were Bulgarian students standing at the barricades instead of sitting in classrooms?

Part of the answer might be found in a seemingly unrelated study. In 2006, Bulgaria was among the worst performing countries participating in the Program for International Student Assessment, an international test that measures academic performance among 15-year-old students. The main focus of the 2006 test was science literacy. With an average score of 434 points, well below the OECD average of 500 points, Bulgaria ranked 44th among 57 countries participating in the program. Bulgarian students had great difficulty answering relatively easy questions such as "What is acid rain?" or "What is the greenhouse effect?"

Both cases are symptomatic of the ailing Bulgarian education system, which simultaneously fails to keep students in the classroom and provide them with the knowledge that they need to succeed outside of school.

Disaffected Teachers

Massive teachers' strikes in the fall of 2007 left Bulgarian classrooms empty for more than a month. Teachers, then earning an average salary of 215 euros per month, were not only protesting for higher salaries, but also for systematic reforms. Increased funding was not the only solution to the problem in many teachers' eyes; in fact, many argued it was nonsensical to pour money into a badly broken system.

Though reform has been the mantra of virtually every government over the past 15 years, without the political will to carry it out, "reform" has become almost a dirty word and, simultaneously, an excuse for inaction. The teachers' strike came as a clear sign that immediate changes were needed.

The concessions teachers won following the strike have fallen well short of their demands.

The government and teachers' unions settled on a cumulative pay increase of nearly 50 percent over a span of 10 months, as well as more education funding in the next budget. The 50-percent increase was well below the 100-percent raise initially demanded, but was viewed by many as a significant victory at the time.

Salary differentiation based upon qualifications, another one of the teachers' demands, went into effect at the beginning of 2008. Educators were also offered additional bonuses for introducing interactive teaching methods into the classroom, organizing extracurricular activities, and encouraging their students' participation in Olympiads and academic challenges.

But the average teacher's salary has yet to reach the 325-euro level that was demanded by striking teachers. Education Minister Daniel Valchev recently said the figure is closer to 300 euros. Many teachers report that they receive much less than that.

Marinela Gospodinova, a German-language teacher at a Sofia middle school, says her net monthly salary is 195 euros. A teacher with 15 years' experience, she was among those striking in the square in front of parliament in 2007, and has been disappointed with developments in the education sphere ever since.

"They have been trying to reform the education system for years now, and every minister starts different reforms. Not a single one, however, has been brought to its conclusion," Gospodinova said.

"I think it's high time to consider education as an investment," said Kameliya Todorova, a teacher at the prestigious First French Language School in Sofia.

At the end of the 2006-2007 academic year, the teachers at Todorova's school decided to protest in a peculiar way: They gave excellent marks (six out of six in the Bulgarian system) to all their students. The protest was an expression of their lack of faith in the current state of education and a way to "fine" the ministry, since the state pays a monetary award to every student with a cumulative grade average of at least 5.50.

"We have protested many times, and achieved no results so far. That's why we decided to use an unusual form of protest this time around," said Todorova.

Some teachers also argue that their low salaries prevent them from staying ahead of the game when it comes to new teaching methods. Marinela Chilikova, who also works at the First French Language School, said: "Every teacher has to be able to afford to pay for their Internet at home and buy new books. With the money we are getting right now, most of us cannot."

New Test Introduced

Valchev survived the strike of 2007 and managed to implement a reform that many of his predecessors had failed at numerous times in the past. In May 2008, high school students across the country sat down to two new standardized final exams at the end of the academic year, called the "matura," one in Bulgarian language and literature, and another on a subject of their choice.

The exams are structured along the lines of the A-Levels in Britain or the French *baccalaureat*, and are prerequisites for those wishing to pursue higher education or other professional qualifications after high school. The standardized exams mean that students' results across the country are now comparable and every student is judged by the same criteria. Supporters of the exams say the new system will also facilitate the comparison of schools and teachers and create an environment of healthy competition among them.

Others are skeptical. Until the new exams were introduced, higher education applicants were judged on their performance during the four or five years they spent in high school. Critics argue that the "matura" exams make those grades redundant and do not motivate students to perform well during their entire secondary school careers.

Moreover, most universities still have their own entrance exams, making the grades on one's own diploma even less valuable. If a student wants to study law or medicine or computer science, he or she still has to take the exam of the corresponding university. However, more universities are expected to recognize the standardized exams as entrance exams when assessing in-coming candidates.

Decentralizing school budgets and delegating rights to school principals to manage their own money are other reforms attempted by the minister of education. They were put in force at the beginning of 2008 under the banner of "The Money Follows the Student."

But decentralizing school budgets has led to tensions in many schools, as principals have tried to save on electricity bills, heating, water, maintenance, work trips, and other expenses so they have enough to pay the salaries of teachers and personnel. Salaries account for some 70 percent of a school's budget.

Yet the new financing system also has the potential to change this bleak picture by increasing competition among schools. Since the state provides an allowance per pupil, the more students a school has, the more money will be injected into its budget.

TOL Chalkboard, 18 February 2009

RUNNING IN PLACE

By Ksenia Pasechnik

Despite efforts to distance itself from Soviet times, the Ukrainian education system can't kick its old habits.

KYIV

Fourteen-year-old Sergey Gusev recently skipped class to play online games in an Internet cafe. His parents, who thought he was in school, believe that their son is a good student. "I don't like chemistry and geometry, so I always miss those lessons," Sergey said casually. He planned to attend only one class that day: physical education.

Sergey is typical of many secondary school students in Ukraine who say they rarely attend their classes because they don't find them interesting. But adolescents' bad attitudes are only one part of the problem. Their lack of motivation is rooted in larger problems in the Ukrainian classroom, including outdated teaching methods, underpaid and uninspired teachers, and a critical lack of resources. And, in a system in which the highest marks often go to the highest bidder, skipping class and avoiding hard work do not necessarily hinder a student's chances for academic success.

Rote memorization remains the norm in Ukrainian schools. Students learn early that they are required merely to reproduce the information drilled into them by their teachers in order to get a good mark. Indeed, many of their exams beginning in primary school are oral.

Maria Gorobets, a high school English teacher in Kyiv, says Ukrainian students are not taught how to think critically about their lessons or to study outside of the classroom. "Education in Ukrainian schools is mechanical," Gorobets said. "All the teachers know it, but they have no motivation to change it because their salaries are low."

A primary or secondary school teacher typically earns the equivalent of

190 euros per month, on par with the national average but still considered relatively low. As a result, many teachers, especially in the regions, leave the profession for higher-paying jobs.

But low salaries are not entirely to blame for the lack of innovation in Ukrainian classrooms. Georgiy Kasianov, director of the education program of the International Renaissance Foundation in Kyiv, sponsored by philanthropist George Soros, said the underlying problem is the absence of autonomy and self-regulation in Ukrainian schools.

Because of Education Ministry requirements, he said, "On the one hand, schools can't work in the manner they consider necessary, and on the other, they can shift responsibility away from themselves for the poor quality of education they deliver." Experts have accordingly identified decentralization as one of the major tasks of education reform in Ukraine.

"I have ideas about how to make lessons much more interesting for my students, but I can't set my lesson plan independently, since I must fulfill the plan set out by the ministry," Gorobets said when asked about her teaching methods.

Private schools have freer rein, but they are only a minority of educational establishments in Ukraine. And studying there is expensive. In Kyiv, one year of private tuition costs approximately 1,500 euros and in the regions it runs to between 530 and 750 euros, making attendance an option available only to Ukraine's elite minority.

Ukraine spends 6.4 percent of its GDP on education, according to the UN Human Development Program, putting it on par with Belarus and even ahead of Poland, but its schools seem woefully underfunded. Working-class parents frequently foot the bill for their children's studies, even in public schools.

Parents often supply the money for repairs or to buy chalk and other basic supplies. Students are forced to buy most of their own textbooks because their schools cannot afford to provide them free-of-charge. This sometimes results in confusion in the classroom, since students will purchase more up-to-date editions that contradict the outdated—and often out-of-print—versions used by their teachers.

Skewing Marks

In 2007, Ukraine implemented standardized examinations for graduating students wishing to go on to higher education. Before, students mostly passed final oral exams and, on the basis of these results, were admitted to universities—a process that was notoriously corrupt. Parents and students were expected to give, and just as often willingly offered, bribes to "pass" these exams.

Now students seeking to attend higher education write a single test covering general knowledge, Ukrainian language and literature, and their chosen specializations. The test is evaluated externally by the Ukrainian Center for Educational Quality Assessment, a state institution charged with managing the process.

Kasianov from the International Renaissance Foundation believes the evaluation of students' knowledge upon leaving secondary school is more objective under the new system. Maybe so, some parents and students say, but it's far from perfect.

"The new system is objective. It checks concrete knowledge," said Marina Egorova, who took the test and graduated this year. But she believes that the format is unforgiving, unlike the previous oral exams: "It doesn't give you a chance to correct your mistakes. If a student doesn't know one date or one place, or makes an error by chance, the result is already bad."

"My son graduated from school this year and took the test. He was always studying and always got good grades in school, but he still did badly," said Svetlana Demchak, the mother of a recent graduate. "The results of one test cannot give an objective evaluation of a student's knowledge," she argued.

Proponents of the new exam say the main benefit is that there are far fewer possibilities for corruption in the university admissions process. While it is still possible for a corrupt teacher to sell the right answers, the fact that the test is evaluated externally removes the teacher's subjective opinions—as well as undue influence—from the equation.

Language Wars

Aside from public opinion, the implementation of the new standardized test has also faced another serious obstacle: the issue of the language of the test itself. Originally, the tests were available only in Ukrainian. However, in response to the demands of officials in mostly Russian-speaking Crimea, as well as heated public protests in that autonomous republic, the ministry announced in January 2008 that it would make the test available in Russian for the next two years, except for the sections on Ukrainian language and literature. After this transitional period, all students will have to take it in Ukrainian even if they study at a minority-language school.

The use of the Russian language in Ukrainian schools is a highly divisive issue. Ukrainian is the official language, though the 1989 Law of Languages and 1996 constitution protect the use of Russian and other minority languages. However, since independence, the education system has been increasingly "Ukrainianized" and the number of Russian-language schools has steadily dropped even in areas where a significant number of Russian speakers remain. Still, in Crimea, around 600 schools continue to teach exclusively in Russian, and in eastern Ukraine, the figure is at nearly 30 percent of all schools.

"My son is studying in Russian and I like it because we only speak Russian at home," said Katerina Lebetskaya, the mother of a secondary school student in Kharkiv, in northeastern Ukraine. "But the problem is that when my son graduates, he'll have to take the [standardized] test in Ukrainian!"

"A few years ago, I could teach in both Russian and Ukrainian as I liked. Students understand both languages," said Irina Shuba, a primary school math teacher in Kremenchug, in central Ukraine. "But now my boss scolds me when I explain something to my students in Russian. The government is trying to raise a 'Ukrainianized' generation."

However, many believe that education should be conducted in the official language of their country. "We live in Ukraine. If someone wants to be educated in Russian, let him go to Russia and study there. In my country, I like my people to speak Ukrainian," said Stefania Savitskaya, a teacher of Ukrainian language and literature in a Kyiv high school.

Diplomas Off the Conveyor Belt

Ukraine has around 300 universities and institutes of higher education, but the quality is low and disconnected from the post-graduation reality faced by students. Students are scarcely acquainted with the demands of their chosen professions because the emphasis in the classroom is on theoretical knowledge over practical skills.

But the blame for the poor output from Ukrainian universities does not lie only with professors and administrators. "The problem is not just the bad quality of education, or the outdated system of teaching, but also the psychology of many students," Kasianov said. Many students go on to higher education simply for the sake of getting a degree, he said, and, as a result, many institutes just "rubber stamp" diplomas.

A series of European reforms, known as the Bologna process, aim to reverse that trend. In addition to restructuring the length and requirements of university programs, the most tangible changes since Ukraine signed on in 2005 have been in the realm of study habits. Now students get points for attending seminars and for carrying out independent tasks outside the classroom. However, the traditional attitude toward learning persists: many students are still oriented toward getting high marks and getting their diplomas, but value the process of learning much less.

Corruption is simultaneously a cause and symptom of this situation. According to Transparency International's 2008 Global Corruption Report, higher education is widely considered one of the most corrupt spheres in Ukrainian life. The report cites a survey conducted the previous year by Management Systems International and the Kyiv International Institute of Sociology in which 47.3 percent of respondents said a bribe was demanded up front in their dealings with universities, while 29 percent said they gave a bribe on their own initiative.

Olga Borovik, a student at the Kyiv Institute of Foreign Affairs, part of the Taras Shevchenko National University, said her parents paid $17,000 four years ago as a bribe upon entering the institute. She said she has frequently had to pay money to her instructors for good marks on exams.

Teachers cite low salaries as the main reason why they are open to bribery. Many students see graft as a mutually beneficial arrangement between teachers and students, a fast and convenient way for them to get ahead in a culture in which bribery is widely tolerated.

Holding On to the Past

The professions being taught in Ukrainian universities and the promotion of numerous obsolete specialties do not match the needs of the contemporary Ukrainian labor market. For example, Igor Kozhevnikov, a former math instructor at Kyiv Polytechnic University, explained that it is possible to get an engineering degree specializing in the production of Keramzit, a lightweight clay compound, but there are virtually no companies left in Ukraine producing this product. On the other hand, there are scarcely enough programs to meet the demand for "modern" professions such as clinical researchers, property agents, and copywriters.

Part of the problem is that instructors in higher education often have a low level of training and professional awareness themselves. Many teachers, from the primary to the university level, received their formal education 10 or 20 years ago and have not updated their qualifications since. There is no movement to force teachers at any level to update their skills.

"The Ukrainian education system has retained its Soviet shape," Kasianov said. "It worked in a mono-ideological system with a centralized economic and social system. But now it is outdated. It needs to be reformed to meet the needs of a mobile market economy, a globalized world, and a fluid society."

Transitions Online, 15 January 2009

WHY SPELLING MATTERS

By Ora Garway

*A Liberian village school's winning words get attention from the
government, but larger problems loom.*

MANGO TOWN, LIBERIA

Golden and draped in red, white, and blue ribbons, the spelling
trophy won by Mango Town School has become more than a source of
orthographic achievement for the students and their teachers. It has brought
a wealth of attention to a school that was largely forgotten.

Before clinching the spelling contest sponsored by the Liberian
government, the primary school was deemed "not conducive" to learning,
according to Principal Joseph Dweh, and had too few textbooks, desks, and
classrooms for its 307 children.

"I mean, we were completely neglected by the government," Dweh
said from his small office in the mud-walled school. "The children's right to
education was infringed upon until we won the spelling bee."

Mango Town School has been around since the 1950s but was
abandoned through much of Liberia's 14-year civil war. The school
reopened in 2005 and has had little attention since.

The Ministry of Education has now vowed to build a new school and
give more attention to Mango Town's needs, Dweh said. The nine teachers,
who had not received their pay for months, also got promises that their
salaries would be paid more regularly.

"Had it not been for the spelling bee that we won, then we would not
have had any attention here," said Varfley Kenneh, a teacher.

Fatu Kamara, 13, a third-grader who participated in the September
2009 spelling contest, also said the trophy has brought changes. "I feel happy
that we were able to win the spelling bee competition, because it made us

start getting textbooks, copybooks, and other things that our friends can receive at their schools."

Daunting Challenges

The trophy notwithstanding, Mango Town is a microcosm of a national education system facing daunting challenges. Liberia has Africa's lowest primary school enrollment rate—30 percent—despite primary school attendance being compulsory since 2006. The net school enrollment rate is 5 percent, according to the government's 2010 Education Sector Plan, and 36 of the nation's 92 districts have no high schools. Net enrollment is based on the number pupils attending classes appropriate to their age.

Girls are more likely than boys to repeat a class, to drop out of school, and to be illiterate, despite concerted efforts to help them and keep them in the classroom. According to recent government health and population surveys, 56 percent of Liberian women never attended school and it is not unusual for high school classes to be overwhelmingly male.

The male-female disparity extends to teaching staffs. Only 3 percent of the nation's high school teachers are women, according to the Education Ministry. Public schools, especially those outside the capital, Monrovia, face a dire shortage of qualified teachers. Most rural schools depend on "volunteers" or "recruits" who have little formal education themselves. Although these teachers are entitled to pay, they are not certified and do not get full civil-service benefits. That means salaries are erratic.

School administrators complain that there is often a disconnect between what the government and international aid groups do, and what schools really need. Teachers and administrators say the national education hierarchy ignores local input when it comes to planning and building facilities.

"Schools are being dedicated in remote areas where there are no students, and there are too many overcrowded schools that have to go begging," said one international aid worker involved in education training and planning. "You can't blame the government entirely because they are trying, but there is just too much of one hand not knowing what the other is doing."

Liberia has faced a monumental task since the civil war ended in 2003, and not just in rebuilding its education system. During the fighting that began in 1990, infrastructure was ransacked, state services were disrupted, and rival warlords looted or destroyed public property. More than half the public schools were ruined, according to Education Ministry.

The fighting left some 200,000 people dead, while an estimated 750,000 Liberians, of a population of 3.5 million, fled to other West African nations. Many have returned, overwhelming a nation that is trying to rebuild schools, infrastructure, and other state institutions.

Backed by generous international support, President Ellen Johnson Sirleaf has made education a priority since taking office in 2006. The Ministry of Education gets the largest allocation from the country's budget—US$43 million this year, or 12.4 percent of public spending. International donors and aid agencies also provide substantial assistance and contributions through school construction and training.

The European Union plans to spend 125 million euros on Liberian education and health through 2013, while the U.S. Agency for International Development alone provided $33.5 million for educational programming in 2010. Plus, 14 American Peace Corps volunteers will take up teaching posts in 2010, returning to the country for the first time since 1990.

When Payday Doesn't Come

Still, school administrators complain of not receiving promised operating funds and non-civil service teachers often say they are not paid for months at a time. Mango Town's Dweh believes that free and compulsory primary education can be realized only if students are encouraged with textbooks, book bags, uniforms, notebooks, and other supplies.

He also said teachers without certificates, currently the backbone of the nation's teacher corps, deserve regular pay. Teachers earn a minimum US$80 monthly.

At Bopolu Central High School in Gbarpolu County in northwestern Liberia, 18 of the 34 staff members are not certified teachers. "Most of the recruited teachers are in the senior high school, so when the teachers are not paid, it affects [the seniors] the most," said John V. Lombeh, the vice principal for instruction.

Teachers are getting frustrated, he said, and looking for other jobs, even in a country where eight in 10 people have little or no work. Bopolu's only high school chemistry teacher left to work for a mining company after going for months without pay. Some teachers fight back—they have launched peaceful demonstrations in Monrovia, and administrators at Bopolu say the instructors sometimes hold back their grades or refuse to go to class to draw attention to their plight. As salaries were being handed out three days before Liberian Independence Day on 26 July, some of the non-civil-service teachers said they had not been paid in five months.

Bopolu, located in a lush countryside of rolling hills four hours' drive north of Monrovia, is accessible only by roads that become rivers of mud during the rainy season. A new classroom block was built this summer so that primary school students could attend class separate from the senior high school located up the hill. But Lombeh worries about having enough teachers as the new academic year starts and says it is nearly impossible to recruit teachers from Monrovia, home of the state university, due to insufficient housing and other inducements.

He also worries about poor sanitary conditions and no water. "It's our biggest challenge," Lombeh said outside his office as sun broke through the dense clouds after a downpour. "There is no water for sanitation … and the cooks have to walk into the village to get water for cooking. We have a water tank but it has a crack and doesn't hold water. We have asked for help, but we still have no water."

Mohammed Kamara, a Bopolu teacher whose children attend the local public school, also worries about how schools are run.

"As a parent you want the children to have quality education," Kamara said. "We don't have that here."

In Mango Town, just off a paved road that leads to Monrovia, school conditions overshadow other problems. There are no toilets, not enough desks, no electricity, and only enough books for every fourth child. "The class is not spacious enough to move around in, the children get dirty fast because of the dirt floor, and the condition of a school also has an effect [on learning]," kindergarten teacher Esther Gweamee said.

Gweamee said she finds it difficult to prepare her lessons in the absence of a curriculum or teaching materials, an acute problem in a country that until last year had only one textbook for every 27 students. "We strain ourselves to find topics to reach to the level of these kids," she said.

Mango Town's principal, Dweh, said his school has not received some government subsidies for two years, meaning he turns to parents and community members for chalk and other materials. When Mango Town School reopened five years ago, the school was so small some classes were held in a village mosque for lack of classroom space. More recently, overflow classes are being held in an unfinished house across the street, with the owner's consent.

Not Doing Their Homework

Some educators say that although the government is trying to improve schools, there are inconsistent and often contradictory policies. Rules are issued and rescinded, and decisions about supplies or construction are made without consulting local districts—problems administrators did not deny in interviews for this article. Principals were told not to hold classes with more than 45 students per teacher, forcing schools to hold two or three shifts a day to accommodate all the students. Teachers who are not qualified in subjects are asked to handle overflow classes.

President Sirleaf in April named a new education minister and deputy minister for instruction after suspending the previous officials in part for the poor conditions at some schools. Since then, the Ministry of Education announced that beginning this academic year, dilapidated schools would not be allowed to operate. But there were no apparently plans to provide temporary classrooms.

"If the government is really serious about that, then I am afraid that they will be denying thousands of children access to education around the country," said Konah Burphy, a teacher in Royesville, Bomi County, west of the capital. "I think what they can do is try to improve the facilities of those schools.

"Some schools do not even have benches for the children to sit on, so they have to carry along with them their seats, they have nowhere to relieve themselves apart from bushes, no safe drinking water at these schools," Burphy said. "These are things that the government needs to start to address instead of saying these schools would not be allowed to operate this school year."

Despite repeated attempts to arrange an interview, Education Minister Othello Gongar could not be reached for comment on educational conditions and policies.

Overcrowding has grown as the government has pushed to expand education as well as retain those in upper grades. School enrollment doubled after the war ended, from 260,499 in 2005 to 539,887 two years later, and continues to grow.

Compounding the overcrowding is a disproportionate number of older students, some over age 20, who missed out on education during the war years or were recruited as marauding fighters and now are going to school. The government has extended its Accelerated Learning Program, designed to compress six years of primary education into three, to accommodate students older than 15. More than 68,000 ALP students were enrolled in 2009 compared with 38,990 in 2005, according to the government's 2010 Education Sector Plan.

Eric Gbah, 19, a senior at the Gray D. Allison High School in Monrovia, said he goes to school as early as 6 a.m. to ensure he gets a seat in the front row of the class. "We were more than 100 last year in the 11th grade. If you are not on campus by that time to secure a seat, then you will have to stand until the end of the school day."

Despite overcrowded conditions in the capital, Montserrado County Superintendent Grace Kpan has announced that she wants all children removed from the streets of greater Monrovia and sent to school when classes start on 1 September. She has already begun running radio programs in the capital region and planned to circulate leaflets to educate parents on the dangers of children in the street, and to instruct families that children should either be in school or at home.

It's Spelled M-A-N-G-O T-O-W-N

At Mango Town School, the principal, teachers, and students are hoping the coming school year will mean a new building, better resources, and regular pay for teachers.

And they are convinced that the spelling trophy, with its ribbons in the national colors, has brought good luck since the students won it on 25 September 2009, defeating a team from a nearby junior high school.

Mango Town School is located in a community of 15,000 in the greater Monrovia region. Opportunity knocked one day when Sirleaf was visiting a nearby privately financed school for children with disabilities—a building shiny with fresh paint, with a water supply, ample desks, and toilets, facilities the public school doesn't have.

According to Dweh, the president's motorcade passed Mango Town School. Dressed in their uniforms, the students went out to greet the president with their spelling trophy and caught her attention. She stopped to greet the students, and that, says Dweh, was the tipping point. After that, the school suddenly got recognition from the Ministry of Education and the district schools chief, and won promises of a new building and a resolution to some of the resource problems.

But efforts to build a new school were held up by a land claim on the school's property, and during the summer break, the school's principal—like those in other rural Liberian primary schools—still had not received some operating funds that were already two years in arrears.

Dweh is confident that Liberia's educational outlook is positive and that more help for his school is coming. But asked how he operates with unpredictable funding, grim conditions, and teachers who sometimes go unpaid, he smiled and said, "By God's grace. By God's grace."

TOL Chalkboard, 30 August 2010

VII. ACHIEVERS

HARD CASES

By *Anita Komuves*

*An alternative high school offers Hungarian
students an unfamiliar feeling—success.*

BUDAPEST

It's hard to say whether the two young men near the entrance to the Belvarosi Tanoda high school are teachers or students. Wearing shorts and T-shirts, they stand chatting, happy that finals are over and summer has arrived.

It turns out one of them is a teacher, the other a student, but the ease of their conversation is no accident. Here, teachers are partners, not superiors, and that's only one way that Belvarosi Tanoda (which means Downtown School and is commonly called BT) stands out from other public high schools.

"Teachers are different here. They're extremely patient, pay attention to you and your problems, and give you as much time as you need if they see some potential in you," says 23-year-old David Strausz, the student.

BT has been working in downtown Budapest for 18 years, helping 16- to 25-year-old high-school dropouts achieve something they had once thought impossible: passing the standardized test that caps the end of Hungarian secondary school studies. The school works with young people with serious problems like addiction or depression, and most of them graduate.

Although its method has often been praised by Hungarian and foreign education specialists, BT is constantly in financial trouble and badly needs a new building. Staff never know if its doors will open the following September.

Invisible People

BT is the brainchild of Edit Gyorik, who had worked with troubled children at a Budapest community center in the late 1980s. Inspired by that experience, and a conference in Canada on drop-out schools, she started setting up BT in a youth center in 1990.

After a year of preparation BT opened and today it is a secondary and technical school that educates around 100 students. It also runs two separate programs, Megallo ("a place to stop") for those with serious substance abuse problems, and Valtosav ("changing lanes") for those incarcerated.

Often, the young people who attend BT have dropped out of not only high school, but the entire institutional care system, Gyorik says. "I can't say, for example, how many of them are Roma or without parents. This isn't important, and these categories are also useless: how do I categorize someone who officially lives with his parents but in fact has not seen them for years and lives alone?" she says. "There is a huge group of young people who are invisible and cannot be reached because all their institutional connections are broken when they drop out of the last school."

The core of the BT method is its complex approach to the students. It seeks not only to teach them but also to help them grow stronger, form a realistic picture of themselves, and re-integrate into society. Teaching is done in small groups where students get individual attention. And unlike in mainstream state schools, each BT student has a personalized learning program: someone might study ninth-grade math but attend 10th-grade history. Groups are reorganized every term according to personal needs and individual development.

"There were times when I was the only one in the class because the teacher was willing to work with me one-on-one. We covered one history book in a week, and I passed the final exam with good results," says Tiziano Tubay, a BT graduate.

Students learn not only the subject matter but also how to take an exam—how to concentrate for hours and write a good draft that helps them during the oral part of the exam. Thus there are exams at the end of every term, and by the time the BT students have to take the *erettsegi*, the Hungarian secondary-school graduation exam, they have a routine and are more confident.

"In BT teachers understood that I wasn't stupid just because I thought differently. Slowly I was able to forget the years of humiliation in my previous schools," says Hanna Cseto, a former BT student who attended two high schools before enrolling there. She is now a college student.

Strausz, the 23-year-old, says, "Once the math teacher explained the same thing six times to someone in the group. The whole class was tired of it, but the teacher was patient even the sixth time. At a normal school that student would have been told to go and take private classes in the afternoon and labeled as stupid."

Tubay, the recent graduate, adds, "Tanoda teaches you that you have a place in this world. It doesn't tell you where that place is, but helps you find it." He has applied to Eotvos Lorand University, Hungary's most prestigious, with plans to major in Hungarian language and literature.

"I only spent my senior year at Tanoda but it had a huge impact on me," Tubay says.

In order to maximize personal attention, every student has a helper among the teachers, with pairs formed at the start of the school year. The student and the teacher meet once a week to discuss whatever concerns the student might have. But this relationship goes deeper than a weekly meeting. Teachers look out for their pairs all the time, and they find time to talk every day. "It should be a relationship based on trust. It might be called a friendship, but every pair has to define the boundaries of the connection. It is a helping situation, and the teacher-helper has to be prepared to accept and cope with the situation if the student starts to treat him or her as a parent or happens to fall in love with him or her," Gyorik says.

Cseto says, "It was very important that I had a partner. If someone hurt me or something bad happened, I could tell her and she helped me with everything. Having a partner does contribute to helping a young person who is, let's say, injured."

In this process the "crew," or staff, helps the teacher-helpers. The teachers gather once a week for an exhausting three- to eight-hour meeting to discuss the students' progress and problems, and ask for help if needed. The crew helps teachers find solutions and acts as a kind of checkup for those who are overwhelmed with work or becoming too closely involved with their students.

"I don't think I could work in a state high school now. I would consider that a step back because I've seen here how the crew works and what kind of relationship teachers can have with the students. I also work in a children's home, and I really miss discussing the cases and helping each other," says Gabor Molnar, who has taught Hungarian language and literature at BT for more than three years.

According to reports filed with the Education Ministry, 149 students attended the school and its Megallo and Valtosav programs in the 2006-2007 academic year. That fall, 31 students sat for the *erettsegi*, or part of it, and another 60 in the spring. Altogether, 37 students graduated.

That figure might seem low, but it is only slightly smaller than the typical size of an "entering class" each September. It's worth remembering, too, that many of those students stood little chance of graduating at their previous schools.

But BT takes on difficult cases, and not everyone succeeds. In 2007, according to the reports, 15 students dropped out of the school, with another six dropping out of the companion Megallo and Valtosav programs. "There are usually at least 40 students who don't come to class regularly or simply disappear," Molnar says. "To tell the truth, there are very few of them who completely drop out. But we wait for all those kids because there comes a time in their life, too, when they come back and realize they want to graduate."

Starved for Cash

The BT method is famous, and it is taught in the pedagogy departments of Hungarian universities. Foreign groups often come to study how the school works. Gyorik received the Education Ministry's and the Soros Foundation's Ottilia Solt Prize last year for outstanding achievement in minority education.

Yet Belvarosi Tanoda, run by its own foundation, is constantly in financial trouble. Students do not pay tuition. As the school provides public services, it is eligible for state funds that cover approximately 30 percent of its costs. Public schools get the remaining 70 percent from their municipality, but BT doesn't. Instead, it gets the free use of its building. To cover the rest of its costs, the school must apply to charities and other donors each year. "We're never sure whether we'll be able to start working the coming September," Gyorik says.

But the money BT needs annually is not much. "We could run

the school on 20 million forints [85,000 euros] a year, but we would be comfortable and happy with twice that amount," she says.

Molnar says, "This is a place where you come to work smiling, though that smile would be wider if our work was rewarded financially. It's harder and harder to make ends meet, and that has an effect on the mood of the crew."

BT's most pressing need is a new, larger space. It sits in downtown Budapest, in a busy and dirty street not far from posh, touristy Vaci Street, on the ground floor of an old apartment building. It was badly damaged by fire in February 2008, so its walls are freshly painted and its furniture is brand new. "All the works of the students that decorated the walls are gone," Gyorik says sadly. "We had just started to feel comfortable," she adds with a bitter laugh.

Although BT has been frequently observed and praised, no other schools have adopted its method. "It's a question of money, but only to a certain extent. Half of it is something else: approach, determination, people. But I'm happy if someone just comes here and then applies one element of the BT method in his own school," Gyorik says. "Imagine how many kids there are in the countryside in the same situation. There could be a school like this in every county, together with a dormitory to help them with accommodation."

Each year more than 100 people apply to BT, but the school can accept only 30 to 40. "The hardest thing to learn was to say no," Gyorik says.

BT is a school for those who need one last chance. Strausz, who has started to do some office work part time at BT while still a student, says, "There are other 'alternative' high schools in the country, but you have to pay tuition there. This is the only place where kids with no money, family, or connections can come."

There are no clear-cut criteria for the admission process, but usually those in the worst situations are accepted, Gyorik says. "Sometimes a big guy, like a politician, makes a call. He has a child in trouble, wants him to finish high school, and heard about BT. I never take those kids because if they still have somebody to make a call for them, an adult to lean on, they're in a much better position than most of our students."

Transitions Online, 6 August 2008

ELECTRONIC REGISTERS CLICK WITH RUSSIAN PARENTS

By Natalia Lazareva

A pilot project allows parents to monitor their children's academic progress through the Internet.

ULYANOVSK, RUSSIA

For many years, Russian schoolchildren have concealed bad grades from their parents with the help of a classic excuse: "My grade report book was taken to be checked."

That excuse may no longer work. Many Russian parents now have the possibility to check up on their child's progress without ever having to leave home or meet with teachers, through the Internet and modern mobile technology.

In July 2008, at a meeting of the State Council Presidium considering the development of an information society in the Russian Federation, President Dimitry Medvedev suggested the creation of electronic school registers and online report cards in addition to paper versions.

Since the beginning of the 2008-2009 school year, the experiment has been conducted in Moscow, Krasnoyarsk, Stavropol and several other cities. One of the most comprehensive programs was launched in the city of Ulyanovsk, some 900 kilometers east of Moscow.

According to representatives of the Education Department in Ulyanovsk, 89 city schools have chosen to participate. At a press conference for the Electronic School Registers project, Ludmila Solomenko, head of the Education Department, said that electronic technology stands to play a greater role in Ulyanovsk's schools in the future. "If the project is successful, this innovation will also be brought to village schools in the Ulyanovsk region," she added.

The electronic register is a paid service, but parents are being asked to sign up for it only on a voluntary basis. For around 60 rubles (less than 2 euros), parents receive a login and a password unique to every pupil. They can access the electronic register at the website "Simbirsk Catalogue," a site on community life in the Ulyanovsk region. (Simbirsk was renamed Ulyanovsk in 1924 to honor its native son, Vladimir Ulyanov, better know as Vladimir Lenin.) The site also hosts pages for participating schools listing their teaching staff, courses, events and news, and allows users to rate the school's sites.

"It is very simple to use: all parents have to do is to agree to a contract with the private company which is in charge of carrying out the project, and they get all the necessary information through their mobile phones or computers," says Svetlana Chikunova, a school accountant. Half of the 60-ruble fee goes to the school as a form of supplementary income and half goes to the company that offers the electronic service.

Not every Russian parent today has access to the Internet, nor sufficient skills to navigate the system. However, as the project leaders predict, the program may help to improve the computer literacy of adults. As of now, around 500 parents in Ulyanovsk, a city of more than 600,000 people, have signed up.

"The idea is very nice," says Larisa Ivanovna, the mother of an eighth-grader, Nastya, with a smile. "At this age, children are sometimes reticent about their successes and failures in school. But now parents are informed about their children's results [without having to ask them]. The information is secure, and teachers are learning how to use these innovative techniques together with us."

The electronic registers caused quite a stir among schoolchildren. "I think it's an awful idea. It distrusts the child and puts pressure on the student!" declared 15 year-old Stas indignantly. But many students admit that this system of supervision fosters a greater sense of responsibility in them.

Homeroom teachers of every class fill in paper registers and deliver them to the school secretary, who in turn uploads the data to the Internet.

Though the project is still in its initial stages, already the lack of coordination at the level of reporting has been pointed to as a major flaw. Some see it as causing twice as much administrative work for teachers. "The electronic register was to supposed to save us from paperwork," complains Elena H., a math teacher in one of the city schools. "Instead of that we have to fill in a pile of paper registers. I spend several hours every day doing this double work. And I get no extra payment for this."

It is too early to tell what the impact of the project will be, though it is a step toward realizing Russia's goal of developing into an information-oriented society. The real benefits and disadvantages of the project will be determined when the project moves from the testing stage to a formalized procedure in Ulyanovsk's schools.

TOL Chalkboard, 19 December 2008

A REVOLUTION LONG IN THE MAKING

By Dorian L. Jones

A program aimed at overhauling teaching practices in Turkey receives kudos, but concerns remain about overcrowding, the dropout rate, and gender disparities.

ISTANBUL

At first glance, the Capa primary school in central Istanbul looks like any typical state school. But beyond appearances, its teachers and students are in the vanguard of a revolution in Turkish education.

For the past five years, Capa has been one of 120 schools across the country piloting a radical initiative, the Support for Basic Education Program. The project, backed by the Turkish government and European Union, aims to change how and what children learn.

In place of traditional methods, in which teachers tend to dictate lessons in a top-down manner, the SBEP scheme encourages two-way engagement. Pupils are now being urged to ask questions of their teachers and think about what they are being taught.

Teaching professionals say the change in approach—and the results— have been dramatic.

"This is a complete transformation in teaching," said Sinan Demir, a grammar teacher at the Capa school. "In the past, it was just about dictating information. Some pupils would understand, while others would just look out the window. But now it is more about helping them to gain skills, improving their communication skills and encouraging them to write creatively. Through these activities we want them to think, question, and reason."

173

The success of the approach is apparent from speaking to Demir's pupils, all of whom were keen to voice their views and recount their experiences.

"We study some subjects by turning them into games or theater plays," said Ayse Gul, 9. "This makes learning all the more entertaining. Before we had to sit silently and the teacher just spoke at us. Now we have to think, and we can talk."

The military coup that unseated the civilian government in 1980 strengthened the long tradition in Turkey of strict school discipline and memorization, an approach that encouraged regimented learning.

The initiative aims to foster a climate of individuality and creative thinking by including special courses for Turkish educators on how to teach "constructively" and place a particular emphasis on interaction with pupils. Some teachers visited European schools, while some European teachers visited their counterparts in Turkey. The exchange phase of the program has ended, but newly trained Turkish teachers are now passing on their skills to other colleagues by visiting schools across the country.

Revisionist History

Much attention has also been focused on the content of lessons, prompting a major review of Turkish textbooks for the 120 schools participating in the SBEP project. The project leader, Anders Lonnqvist Thorsten, originally of Finland, said this was among the initiative's most sensitive tasks—requiring tact and a diplomatic approach. "We are not saying it has to be like this or like that. In Finland, we would not like people from Russia or Sweden or England saying, 'This is what you should teach,'" he said. "It is a national issue. All we are doing is giving ideas."

Along with revising textbooks to make lessons more interactive, the content is also in the process of transformation. For example, the strong nationalist discourse in history books—in particular, strident criticism of neighboring Greece, Turkey's long-time rival—has been modified. A similar project in Greece to revise its strategy for teaching history in relation to Turkey has also begun.

Even more sensitive subjects, such as religion, have been excluded. At present, a separate Turkish-EU initiative is working on the issue of religious education. The EU has commissioned several leading academics to write papers on teaching religion in schools, which is compulsory in Turkey. Strong criticism of religious education has long emanated from some quarters in Turkey, perhaps most loudly from the country's large Alevi community. Alevis, who comprise up to 25 percent of the population, have a different interpretation of Islam, widely considered more moderate than orthodox Islam. They claim schools are only teaching the Sunni branch of Islam.

An Alevi family successfully won a discrimination case in the European Court of Human Rights in October 2007. Further cases are pending. The government says religious textbooks have now been revised to cater to Alevi beliefs.

But Professor Istar Gozaydin of Istanbul Technical University, who has compiled a report for the EU on religious education, argues that such reforms are not enough. "There needs to be a change in the mentality in the way religion is taught. Today, religious education teaches the Sunni belief as a theology, rather than [offering] a study of various beliefs and morals." With the ruling Justice and Development Party having Islamic Sunni roots, the issue remains extremely contentious in Turkish society.

The question of education in the languages of national minorities has also raised tensions, especially in regard to Turkey's substantial Kurdish population, accounting for nearly 20 percent of the country's 78 million people. Claiming discrimination, the country's main Kurdish party, the Democratic Society Party, has campaigned for Kurdish to be used in all levels of education. The government, however, has dismissed their demands out of hand. Similar to their predecessors, the authorities have strictly enforced the principle that there is only one official language in Turkey.

Kemal Kirisci, a professor of international relations at Bosphorus University, says that such rigidity is born out of the fear that Turkey faces the threat of disintegration: "When you scratch the surface of a Turk, underneath you find very quickly that there are many who are descendants of Bosnians, Tartars, Turks from the Balkans, Pomaks, maybe Arabs in the southeast, Kurds certainly. Such a social composition does generate concerns among officials and some of the public that if one group is given special status, then the next step will be others seeking it too," Kirisci said.

But the Democratic Social Party is looking to the EU for support. Richard Howitt, a British member of the European Parliament, said in

Istanbul that he expects the right to Kurdish-language education will be raised when the membership chapter on cultural rights is opened as part of Turkey's EU ascension process.

If the debate on minority education makes it to Brussels, it would likely further complicate the already up-and-down relationship between the EU and Turkey. EU officials have lauded the SBEP's role in helping to break down Turkish suspicions toward Europe, an attitude fostered by Turkey's laborious EU-membership negotiations.

"Very often, the negotiation process is perceived perhaps as us [the EU] against Turkey," said EU Ambassador Marc Pierini, at the opening of a school in Istanbul's Arnavutkoy district earlier this year. "This is not the case. I mean, this is us together. We are going to make a deliberate effort to demonstrate to people that we are working together to achieve this objective."

Most of the 100 million euros earmarked for the five-year SBEP project has been spent building new schools in deprived areas.

Nominally Free Education

SBEP's initial five-year phase finished at the end of 2007, when the initiative was extended from the 120 pilot projects to all of Turkey's primary schools. It has also been used as a model for World Bank-funded projects in Turkish secondary schools and adult education, which also aim to encourage more interaction between teachers and pupils. A major revision of all textbooks has also begun.

Experts also say that adapting the SBEP project to secondary schools makes sense because curricula and teaching methods are most in need of an overhaul at this level. Chronic overcrowding remains a major concern and, with 50 percent of Turkey's population under the age of 25, the demand for education is unlikely to abate. It is not uncommon for schools to provide education for one group of children in the morning and a second group in the afternoon.

Increasingly, primary and secondary schools are coming under fire for charging parents for education. Although tuition is nominally free, many schools now demand payment for a child's registration. Principals claim the payment is necessary to make up shortfalls in funding, especially for the maintenance of buildings. But the Turkish media regularly uncover

176

scandals involving the misuse of such funds. Parents also complain about the rising cost of secondary school textbooks and writing paper that they must purchase for their children.

The increasing financial burden of sending children to school is leading to reports of a rising dropout rate, mainly in secondary schools. The problem is particularly acute in rural areas, where many older children work the fields to supplement the family income. It also disproportionately affects girls, both at the primary- and secondary-school level, with older girls sometimes also dropping out to get married.

Over the past few years, UNICEF, the World Bank, and the Turkish Education Ministry have launched various programs designed to increase female school attendance. Some activities have featured celebrities, including the Turkish female pop icon Sezen Aksu, and corporate sponsors also provided financial assistance. One project offers a monthly 22-euro stipend to the poorest families for each girl sent to school. Around 100,000 payments are currently being made. The Education Ministry reported in 2007 that the gap between boys' and girls' attendance had been narrowed from 25 percent to 10 percent, and almost 225,000 more girls are now enrolled.

Slow to Change

Despite these steps forward, the quality of Turkish education remains a drawback. The Education Ministry's Project Coordination Center identified several problems, particularly in teacher training, while assessing the SBEP scheme's application to the country's 35,000 primary schools.

"We have received complaints and criticism from some teachers about the level of training—some have struggled to adapt," said Ozgul Tortop of the Project Coordination Center. "But that is not surprising. We are talking about 100,000 teachers and this is the first year. It will take time."

The center is encouraging such feedback and has created a portal on its webpage for teachers to voice their views. The EU, meanwhile, is conducting an impact assessment, and its findings will be vital to shaping the project's future. An EU official said after the findings of the study have been analyzed further funding will be allocated, in co-ordination with Turkish government financial support.

"The impact assessment is crucial in helping us decide where we go from here. It is a learning process for all of us," Mustafa Balci, head of education at the EU's office in Ankara.

Back at the Capa school, Sinan Demir is both exhausted and exhilarated at the end of a long school day. The new system is far more demanding, he admits, but the rewards outweigh any feelings of tiredness. "I have waited my entire career to be able to teach like this," he said. "This is what teaching is about—that you can come to a point with a child where they believe they can do whatever they aspire to."

Demir spent his summer touring the country to educate fellow teachers about the new curriculum. Many of the problems Turkey faces are blamed, at least in part, on lingering military-style teaching methods. With this pioneering scheme, hope now exists that the next generation will be able to resolve them.

TOL Chalkboard, 14 December 2008

A SECOND CHANCE

By A'Eysha Kassiem

*Adult education is on the upswing in South Africa, as generations
that lost out on schooling under apartheid head back to class.*

ATLANTIS, SOUTH AFRICA

It's Monday morning and Anne Loock is awake and ready for school.
She goes over her math homework, packs a pencil box, and heads out the
door.

"Afrikaans is my favorite subject," she beams. "Especially reading and
writing essays."

But Anne is not the typical pupil. For the past year and a half, this
great-grandmother, who is 70 years old, has been learning how to read and
write.

"I was never able to go far with school," Loock says. "During those
years, it was a difficult time. I was 12 years old when I had to go and work
and help my mother on a farm. At the time, the emphasis was not on school.

"But now I understand the value of having an education," she says.

As one of the oldest learners at the Adult Education and Training
Center in Atlantis—a small, impoverished community in the Western Cape,
about 40 kilometers from Cape Town—Loock is part of a growing number
of adult learners in the area who have chosen to get the education they
never had. Faced with poverty and unemployment in a community that
was marginalized during apartheid, adult learners with minimal education,
or those who never finished their final year (Grade 12), have found it
increasingly difficult to compete in the new South Africa.

Prior to the end of South Africa's official segregation policies in
1994, schools and students were divided and classified by race. The Bantu
Education Act of 1953 ensured that more money was spent on the white

minority. Schools that catered to the black, Indian, and colored communities were largely structured in a way that led to non-white pupils receiving a substandard education, ensuring that these communities would remain downtrodden by leaving them unskilled.

The Atlantis Adult Education and Training Center is located in the heart of the community—a small, rundown building surrounded by neighboring, state-run primary and high schools, where uniformed children play seemingly unaware of the privilege that their older peers must envy.

The government-funded center caters to some 400 adults with levels from a primary education through Grade 12. Institutions such as the Atlantis center have spread throughout the country. In the Western Cape Province alone—where Atlantis is located—some 36,000 students are enrolled at 295 sites.

Education officials believe continued schooling can reduce adult illiteracy rates and bridge the gap caused by apartheid.

"We hope that those who have been disadvantaged in the past are provided with a second chance to empower themselves and in so doing, uplift the community as well as the nation as a whole," said Jaywant Parbhoo, senior curriculum planner for Adult Education and Training Assessment at the Western Cape Province Education Department.

In November, for the first time, the national Education Department will ensure these students who have gained competency in basic education receive a new qualification, the General Education and Training Certificate. That will allow them to take courses at the college or university level.

Catching Up

Loock, a pensioner, has been living in Atlantis for 34 years, and until 2009, had never learned to read and write.

"A friend of mine who is also in her 70s invited me to come to class with her one day. She motivated me, so I enrolled in the Grade 2 class. We did subjects such as health and math and learned how to read and write essays. It was hard, but I passed the year, so I came back to learn more," she says, smiling frequently.

Another student, 46-year-old Deborah Moses, can relate. She is unemployed, but recently received her Grade 12 certificate from the center—28 years after first leaving school. She lives in Atlantis with her youngest son and her sister, the family's breadwinner.

"Apartheid played a huge role in why I left school at the end of Grade 10," Moses says. "I couldn't even get an admin job because it was only the whites who could get those jobs. ... I need my final-year certificate to get a job, and I hope having it will change my situation."

Moses, who hopes to be employed as a librarian, says many of her classmates are older than she is.

"We encourage each other. When someone fails, we encourage him or her to keep trying," she says. "I motivate as many young people as I can about completing school and getting their matriculation [Grade 12 qualification] because it's so much harder when you're older.

"But I made it when I thought I couldn't do it. I'm proud of myself and excited. I believe there is a job for me out there. There will be."

Her history teacher at Atlantis is Neville De Waal. Although a full-time teacher at neighboring Robinvale High School, De Waal teaches at the adult center at night.

"It's nice to teach older learners," he says. "I can actually enjoy myself. Learners at schools aren't serious about schooling, but these older learners are. I think it's because education and Grade 12 means so much more to them."

De Waal says his colleagues at the high school often ask why he takes on the extra workload. "It's my part of giving back to the community. These learners know why they are here and are really committed," he says. "There are normally a lot of women who come to my class straight from their jobs and that impresses me. Some of the learners are even older than I am, and it's difficult sometimes wondering how I ought to address them."

But a class with varying levels of learning comes with its obstacles.

"Some of the learners struggle with reading. I can't always give them homework to do because I know they don't have the time, and because they don't have books, I normally copy texts from books to teach them," De Waal says.

Shareen Hart, the center manager, says she is inspired by the students everyday. Hart has been running the center for the past 10 years and says that, despite the majority of students being unemployed, the center has an annual Grade 12 pass rate as high as 93 percent.

"Sometimes, you have people coming here who only want to learn how to write their names or they just want to be able to read their Bible. But then they realize the value and they don't want to stop there," Hart says. "They can see how education can make a difference." Being able to write one's own name rather than simply marking a cross gives her students a sense of dignity, she says.

"People here are really starting to see how education empowers you and especially with the recession, they see there's definitely a need to better their skills to give their families a better living."

Celebrity Students

Hart says that even well-known people in the community who never finished school have come forward to attend classes. "At first they are embarrassed because people don't know [that they didn't graduate]," she said. It is especially difficult for these community leaders to admit to their lack of education. "But I have so much respect for these learners— especially the elderly ones—and that motivates me and makes me grateful."

"Learners here don't even know if they are going to have [food] to eat before they come to class," Hart adds.

Her oldest students know all too well the challenges of starting to study again.

"It's not easy," says Loock. But whenever she feels like giving up, she realizes she has already come so far.

"If it goes well, I think I will keep going on with my studies this year," she says. "I feel healthy enough and want to do something that makes me feel like I can talk to people [about things that matter] rather than sitting quietly because I don't know enough to have anything to say.

"For me, at 70 years old, finally being able to participate feels nice."

TOL Chalkboard, 12 November 2010

EVOLUTION WILL HAVE TO DO

By *Sabina Arlsanagic*

Though not a revolution, reforms are gradually making Bosnia's schools less politicized and authoritarian.

SARAJEVO

Nadja Steta was among the teachers of the first generation of children starting the first grade under a new law that extended mandatory schooling to nine years. That was in 2004, and she still remembers having "panicked" because of the task ahead.

"The new requirements put us under a lot of strain, but I think that the reforms introduced so far are really good," said Steta, who teaches in the Bosnian capital. "Children have been placed at the center of attention in classrooms—unlike in the past when teachers were the undisputed authority."

Those reforms, the product of an education bill adopted in 2003, led to inevitable growing pains but have emerged as a turning point in the development of the country's education system. And while most experts agree that ethnic divisions still weigh heavily in Bosnia—coloring the teaching of numerous subjects such as history, geography, and religion— there is some hope that reforms that encourage independent and creative thinking could lead students and their parents to start questioning the country's divisive education policies.

A Watershed Law

Spurred on by the Organization for Security and Cooperation in Europe, the 2003 law prescribed the statewide introduction of nine-year, mandatory primary education to replace the previous eight-year program, allowing for school enrollment one year earlier, at the age of 6. That change was an important step in a country where the preschool attendance rate stands at around 7 percent but is closer to zero in most rural areas.

The new law also called for an innovative style of teaching to replace lecture and memorization. Now teachers must provide more task-based class sessions and tailor their teaching style and grading decisions to the needs and abilities of students. Pupils are encouraged to engage in their own research and to discuss and debate. The law also opened the way for the integration of children with special needs into the general school population.

For the first few years, the situation was trying for many teachers, who would receive their teaching plans and program just a couple of weeks before the start of the school year. Suddenly, they were expected to invest a considerable dose of their own creativity in coming up with teaching aids to engage 6-year-olds.

"Things have started improving now," Steta said. "Textbooks are being polished; teaching plans are prepared in advance. We still lack resources to introduce proper teaching aids, but reforms take time," she said. "In a financially constrained, postwar society such as ours you cannot expect miracles to happen overnight."

Marina Mesanovic, also a primary-school teacher in Sarajevo, agrees that the reforms were necessary to accommodate new generations of children and young parents who "live faster, who are curious, who have access to the Internet, and can find knowledge everywhere."

However, Mesanovic, who teaches math and physics, said the authorities have not given teachers the training they need to prepare them for the new requirements, in particular for work with disabled children.

Tough Assignment

Mesanovic teaches three classes of 30 children each, including seven children with learning difficulties and special needs.

"It's very difficult because nobody prepared us to work with children with special needs, and we also still teach to groups of 30 children without teaching assistants," she said.

"Some of these children need help with going to the toilet. They need to take breaks in the middle of a lesson. ... Integration is generally a wonderful idea, but someone should have thought about how to make it work," she said.

Funding for modern teaching equipment is also lacking. "Chalk and the blackboard remain our main teaching tools," Mesanovic said.

Similar complaints, particularly about the insufficiency of teacher training, are heard across the country.

"Most teachers I know have attended some seminars to get acquainted with new, interactive, and child-focused approaches to teaching," said Gordana Kecman, a primary school psychologist from Banja Luka. But Kecman says the country lacks a systematic approach to teacher training. "We have no accredited teacher-training program to help teachers gain new skills and upgrade their qualifications."

Aleksandra Ukoljac, from the Banja Luka-based nongovernmental organization Hi Neighbor, said that when teachers in her city were required to pass special computer literacy exams, many had to turn for help to their students to prepare.

"But you cannot blame teachers for that," Ukoljac said. "The training programs that the authorities provide are mostly theoretical and don't help them gain practical skills."

While some accept the government's excuse that the global recession has further diminished already scarce funding, others believe that the problems stem from skewed priorities.

Some critics, such as Berina Hamzic, from the Sarajevo-based nongovernmental organization Our Children, complained that the authorities spend a large chunk of the budget on social handouts, mostly to war veterans, but are shy when it comes to investing in education.

"Last year, the government of the Sarajevo region announced there would be no public funding available to support NGOs, but only days later they published a call for funding of projects to assist war veterans and demobilized soldiers," she said. "It's just an example of how they are more willing to invest in the past than in the future."

Sarajevo is in the Bosniak-Croat Federation, one of the two semi-autonomous parts of the country. Over the past four years, the federation government has been spending up to 40 percent of its budget on welfare payments to war veterans and families of soldiers killed in the 1992-1995 war.

By comparison, it's nearly impossible to know how much is spent on education in the federation, as the central administration funds only its own Education Ministry salaries and some textbook and other minimal capital purchases. Most of the money for schools comes from the budgets of the federation's 10 cantons.

A New Voice in Schools

One area where the law has clearly led to tangible change, despite the funding problems, is the growing power of student and parent councils. With the establishment of these councils, also mandated by the 2003 education law, children and their parents were given a say in the work and life of the country's schools.

Among other things, council representatives sit on school boards and represent the interests of students and parents on a wide range of issues, from the choice of meals to the introduction of educational, volunteer, or cultural activities.

Supported by Save the Children Norway, Hi Neighbor joined forces with Our Children three years ago to set up student-teacher groups in 18 schools across the country to monitor how children's rights are respected, including access to education by minorities and other vulnerable groups.

Monitoring reports prepared by these groups have often triggered debate among school management, teachers, students, and parents, and sometimes to tangible results, such as the purchase of new equipment, the introduction of special after-school activities, and the organization of tolerance-promoting campaigns.

While some teachers and school boards still fail to understand that they must allow children and their parents to challenge them and to actively engage in the work of the schools, guidance counselor Jadranka Kapetanovic said those attitudes are changing. She points to the example of parents of children with special needs, who are pushing schools to adopt the necessary changes to accommodate their children.

Kapetanovic is herself involved in the work of one such group and encourages parents to write letters not only to school management but also to the local authorities to demand extra support because many schools still cannot afford to hire special education experts, psychologists, or medical staff. Schools also lack funding for special teaching aids, such as textbooks for visually impaired children.

"Slowly and with a lot of difficulty, some things are changing. The voices of parents and children are increasingly being heard," she said.

Challenging the Status Quo

Other parents have started to feel empowered enough to challenge lingering segregation in the education system, which continues to reflect political and ethnic divisions caused by the 1992-1995 war.

A weak central government presides over the Serb-dominated Republika Srpska and the Bosniak-Croat Federation. The federation's 10 cantons have their own regional governments, most of which are dominated by either Bosniaks or Croats.

As a result, Bosnia's education system is governed by 13 authorities set up for different parts of the country.

Numerous internationally sponsored efforts to integrate the system have borne little fruit due to opposition by nationalists who remain in power 15 years after the war's end.

While Bosniak (Bosnian-Muslim), Croat, and Serb children continue to be taught different and mostly conflicting interpretations of history, geography, language, and literature, some parents have started questioning the status quo.

The Association for Parent-School Cooperation, which includes some 1,200 parents from across Bosnia, recently launched a program to challenge the official view that disbanding the so-called "two schools under one roof" approach is impossible.

Proposed by the OSCE at the end of the war, these schools were meant to be a temporary solution for providing education to children who returned to their prewar homes in areas subjected to ethnic cleansing. But today more than a dozen such schools still exist, where children from different ethnic groups use the same building but are taught different things, by different teachers, from different textbooks—all the while physically separated from one another.

The parents association went to these schools and involved children, parents, and teachers from all ethnic groups in community projects.

"Regardless of their ethnic background, they all worked together to improve conditions in their schools," said Samir Haljeta, a coordinator for the group. "Serbs, Croats, and Bosniaks worked together to, for example, stock their school libraries."

As part of the project, children from ethnically divided communities jointly participated in art classes, sports competitions, and roundtables on issues such as drugs and human trafficking.

"We want to actively engage in schools. We want to democratize schools; we want to exclude politics from education, including from the appointment of teachers and school boards," Haljeta said. "A significant number of parents, children, and education professionals all want the same thing, but politics obstructs efforts to achieve these goals."

Aleksandra Jankovic, an education adviser in the Bosnian mission of the OSCE, sounded cautiously optimistic.

"Improving the education process and empowering children, teachers, and parents might be a good way to achieve changes in education policy," she said. "Over time, this could lead to a situation where the authorities will be forced to respond to the needs of children and parents instead of using educational policy to force their political discourse on them."

"That moment has not come yet," Jankovic said. "But in some aspects, the situation is developing in the right direction, and I believe that it is possible for real change to come from the bottom up."

TOL Chalkboard, 16 August 2010

CONTRIBUTORS

Farrukh Akhrorov heads the Media Group and Mercy journalists' organization in Tajikistan.

Sabina Arlsanagic is a Sarajevo-based journalist and regular contributor to Balkan Insight and other media.

Claudia Ciobanu is a reporter for Inter Press Service.

Sinziana Demian is a writer for *Formula AS* magazine in Bucharest.

Ljubica Grozdanovska Dimishkovska is TOL's correspondent in Skopje.

Jeremy Druker is executive director of Transitions and editor in chief of Transitions Online.

Barbara Frye is managing editor of Transitions Online.

Ora Garway is managing editor of *Punch*, a biweekly newspaper in Monrovia, Liberia.

Andrea Gregory is an American journalist writing a book about women's rights in Serbia.

Bakyt Ibraimov is a freelance journalist in Kyrgyzstan.

Dorian L. Jones is an Istanbul-based journalist and radio documentary producer.

A'Eysha Kassiem is a South African journalist and writer based in Cape Town.

Lucie Kavanova is a journalist in the Czech Republic.

Tamar Kickacheishvili is a reporter for *Georgia Today*, an English-language newspaper in Tbilisi.

Anita Komuves is TOL's correspondent in Budapest.

Wojciech Kosc is a TOL correspondent in Poland.

Onnik Krikorian is a freelance photojournalist and writer based in Yerevan. He is also the Caucasus region editor for Global Voices Online and writes from Armenia for the Frontline Club.

Natalia Lazareva is a Russian and Chuvash journalist based in Ulyanovsk. Her article was produced as an assignment for the Improving Coverage of Education Issues online course organized by TOL and developed in cooperation with the Guardian Foundation and the BBC World Service Trust, with support of the Open Society Foundations' Education Support Program.

Maysam Najafizada is an Afghan journalist who has written for BBC Monitoring and *Der Spiegel*.

Tanya Obushtarova is a journalist with the *Kapital* weekly in Sofia.

Athar Parvaiz is a journalist based in Srinagar.

Ksenia Pasechnik is the editor of *Excise* magazine in Kyiv.

Ruzanna Rashidgizi is a Baku-based journalist.

Animesh Roul is the executive director of the New Delhi-based Society for the Study of Peace and Conflict.

Talant Sadykov is a pseudonym for a Kyrgyz journalist.

Lena Smirnova is the pseudonym of a journalist based in Uzbekistan.

Timothy Spence is a freelancer and journalism trainer based in Vienna and Maastricht, Netherlands. He was managing editor of Transitions Online in 2007 and 2008.

Galina Stolyarova is a writer for *The St. Petersburg Times*, an English-language newspaper.

Pavol Szalai covers foreign affairs for *SME*, a daily newspaper in Slovakia.

Hamid Toursunov is TOL's correspondent in Osh, Kyrgyzstan.

Olesya Vartanyan is a reporter for Radio Free Europe/Radio Liberty's service for South Ossetia and Abkhazia.

Boyko Vassilev is a moderator and producer of the weekly *Panorama* news talk show on Bulgarian National Television.

Vishaka Wehella is a freelance writer and media trainer who helped establish the Sri Lanka Women Journalists Network.

Farruh Yusupov is a correspondent for the Uzbek-language service of Radio Free Europe/Radio Liberty in Prague.

PHOTO CREDITS

Chapter I
Red Army sappers at Leningrad, 1941. British official photo, RR-154. United States Library of Congress, LC-USZ62-25900.

Chapter II
An officer of the UN Observer Mission with children in Georgia's Abkhazia region, 2005. United Nations photo by Michal Novotny.

Chapter III
Primary school students in Darvari, Romania, 2009. UNESCO photo by Petrut Calinescu.

Chapter IV
A student erases the classroom blackboard in Harar, Ethiopia, 2003. United Nations photo by Eskinder Debebe.

Chapter V
A Serbian student reads a book on the rights of children, 2010. OSCE photo by Milan Obradovic.

Chapter VI
Guie Town School, Liberia, 2010. Photo by Timothy Spence.

Chapter VII
Students in Tarnabod, Hungary, from the Roma Decade's Chachipe Youth Photo Contest, 2008. Photo by Janos Kummer.

FOOTNOTES

1. 27 January 2009.
2. Aida Ramusovic, TOL's correspondent in Podgorica, contributed to this report.
3. This was one in a series of articles published by Transitions Online in 2009 to mark the 20th anniversary of the collapse of communism in Eastern Europe.
4. Iasi is a city in eastern Romania.
5. Following months of frustration over rising prices and government cronyism, violence erupted in Kyrgyzstan in early April 2010 leading to the ouster of Kurmanbek Bakiev from the presidency. But the unrest also unleashed methodical attacks on the ethnic Uzbek minority, whose entrepreneurial acumen had created frictions with the Kyrgyz majority, especially in the southern regions bordering the Ferghana Valley.
6. Ibid.
7. Pass percentage represents the percentage of students who manage to continue on to the next grade.
8. Armenian prosecutors dropped the case against Sukhudyan shortly after the U.S. ambassador to Armenia, Marie L. Yovanovitch, presented her with the Woman of Courage Award on 10 March 2010 in recognition of Sukhudyan's civic work.
9. Chudinov was replaced by Roza Otunbaeva, also the interim president, in April 2010.
10. Crimean Tatars, who represent less than 1 percent of Ukraine's 46 million people, trace their roots to Turkic peoples of Anatolia and Central Asia who settled the region more than six centuries ago.
11. Yushchenko was president of Ukraine from 2005 to 2010.

ABOUT TRANSITIONS

TRANSITIONS is a nonprofit organization established to strengthen the professionalism, independence and impact of the news media in the post-communist countries of Europe and the former Soviet Union. Based in Prague, the organization does this through a combination of journalism and media training programs, and the publication of Transitions Online (www.tol.org) magazine.

Training journalists and other media professionals in the post-communist region has always been a key part of the Transitions mission. Transitions runs a variety of programs—residential, distance learning, seminars, internships and coaching—with two main aims: to offer practical journalism training, and to help participants either improve existing media outlets or set up new ones.

The Transitions Online Internet magazine covers political, social, cultural, and economic issues in the former communist countries of Europe and Central Asia. It has a strong network of contributors, who provide valuable insight into events in 29 countries.